TEA

A 30-Day Devotional

Andria Singletary

Cover Design: Vision 2 Life Corporation

A Note to Readers

Please note that this book should not be used in lieu of professional medical care or treatment. Readers should consult with their doctor or other qualified health professionals prior to implementing any of the teas discussed in this book into your daily diet. The information in this book is intended to introduce readers to selected teas as herbal remedies. These natural remedies should first be discussed with your healthcare provider. This book is not to be used in place of medical advice given by a trained medical professional. All health conditions and treatments should be discussed with a doctor or other qualified health professional. The author does not assume any liability for any possible consequences from any treatment or action by any person reading or applying the information in this book.

Dedication

This book is dedicated to the One who gave me the strength, wisdom, and creativity to complete this book. If it was not for my Lord and Savior, Jesus, I would not be able to share this amazing book with you all. He honestly stayed on me about finishing this book. Even when year after year would pass by and this book was not completed, He would constantly remind me of the importance of finishing this book. Thank You Lord for using me to share this great message.

I would also like to dedicate this book to my incredible husband. Thank you for always supporting my dreams and for letting me hog your computer when my laptop quit on me. I love you baby and I am so grateful for your constant encouragement. You da best!

Lastly, this book is dedicated to my incredible parents. Mommy and Daddy, you have both been my support system since the very beginning. You both have encouraged me to always achieve my goals. Thank you for always pushing me to further my education. It was honestly through my schooling that I discovered my passion for writing. I love you both dearly.

Acknowledgements

First, I would like to say thank you to Chanel E. Martin. Chanel, I know I have said this to you quite a few times but thank you again for creating your group Write with Me. It was in this group that I was motivated to finish my first book. It was in this group that I was showered with so much love and encouragement. Chanel, you have truly been a blessing! I would also like to thank Nicholas Bartley of Vision 2 Life Corporation. Thank you for bringing to life my vision for my book cover.

Contents

Introduction 1

Day 1: Tunnel Vision 5

Day 2: Your Thoughts Towards Others 10

Day 3: The Comparison Game 15

Day 4: Forgiveness. Is it Necessary? 20

Day 5: Be Still. 25

Day 6: Peace that Surpasses All Understanding 30

Day 7: God Opportunities 35

Day 8: But What About Me Lord? 40

Day 9: The Power of Our Words 45

Day 10: Does God Care About the Small Stuff? 50

Day 11: How Do You Handle Criticism? 55

Day 12: A Season of Relentless Storms 60

Day 13: Shut the Flesh Up! 65

Day 14: Anchor of My Hope 69

Day 15: Loving as Christ Loves Us 74

Day 16: Taking Matters Into Our Own Hands 79

Day 17: Same Body, Different Callings 84

Day 18: Awaiting a Response 89

Day 19: Living a Life of Excellence 94

Day 20: Righteousness 99

Day 21: Patience in Affliction 104

Day 22: Consistency 109

Day 23: Knowing Abba's Voice 113

Day 24: What Are Your Eyes Seeing? 118

Day 25: Jealousy 124

Day 26: Thinking We Know More Than God 129

Day 27: Fumbling Through the Dark 135

Day 28: God, My Helper 140

Day 29: A Root of Bitterness 144

Day 30: Responding to God's Promises 149

References 154

Index 167

About the Author 172

INTRODUCTION

Writing *Tea for Two* has been a long journey for me. When this journey first began in 2015, it was met with an empty road and smooth cruising ahead. Those empty roads were soon filled with bumper-to-bumper traffic called life. Between meeting my now husband in 2015, finishing graduate school in 2016, going on my first mission trip, starting a new career, planning a wedding all in 2017, getting married and figuring out how to balance life with my career in 2018, writing this book happened sporadically over the past four years. I will be honest, there were times when I lacked the motivation and energy to write. There were times when I forgot my "why" for writing this book. And there were times when life just happened. Despite the twists and turns and the unexpected hindrances that came my way, Jesus would not let up on me about writing this book.

Maybe I'm exaggerating, but I feel like every time we would spend time together in His Word, prayer, or worship, I could hear Him telling me, "So Andria, when do you plan on finishing *Tea for Two*?" Finishing this book and walking in obedience to my Lord and Savior has given me a peace like never before.

The idea for *Tea for Two* first came to me four years ago, back when I was an avid blogger. My blog was filled with inspirational and encouraging posts. These posts were birthed from scripture and revelation I would receive during my one on one time with Jesus. One day I was reading through my previous blog posts and the thought dawned on me, "Wow...these posts could actually be daily devotionals." In that moment, I knew I had a book in the making. I started with the blog posts I had previously written. I refined and shortened the posts to fit more of a devotional format. I then did what I always did, which was spent my quiet time with Jesus and allowed Him to minister to me.

Through these intimate moments with Jesus, I was given great revelation to use for the remainder of my book. When I first began writing *Tea for Two*, I drank coffee religiously. My daily meetings with Jesus frequently included a hot cup of joe. Now most wouldn't have considered me a true coffee drinker. See, my coffee was more of a whole lot of hazelnut creamer with a little bit of coffee. That was the only way I could drink it. All of that changed at some point while writing *Tea for Two*. Dear old joe was not doing it for me anymore. My cup of joe no longer gave me that "umph" like it once did during my grad school years and I needed to pull an all-nighter. If anything, it made me more tired than I was upon waking. That's when I turned to tea.

My first true experience with tea happened to be at Starbucks of all places. Someone had recommended Starbucks Chai Tea Latte and so I decided to give it a try. It was love at first taste...or sip. I was hooked immediately. I never knew that tea could be so delicious and invigorating.

I had found my new addiction, and thus began my new adventure: an exploration of teas and their many health benefits. I wanted to learn more about teas and how they could be used to treat various health issues. One of my "health issues" at the time was insomnia. I was not officially diagnosed, but every night I would be wide-awake when I should have been sleeping like a baby. I was a night owl. I'm not sure if this was due to my countless all-nighters during my college years or my brain simply did not know how to go into sleep mode. After some research, I discovered the amazing benefits of Chamomile tea. After my first cup of Chamomile tea, I could not believe that I had actually fallen asleep at a decent hour. I then began to think to myself again. I wondered how many people were missing out on countless hours of sleep because they did not know about Chamomile tea. That's when I decided that I had to share this information in my book. But how? That's when Jesus gave me the idea for *Tea for Two*.

The purpose of Tea for Two is to cultivate both your spiritual and physical health. The daily devotionals are written to push you closer to God. Intimate moments with Him are so precious. It is during these times that we hear the Lord most audibly. It is during these times that His gentle whispers bring us the calm and peace we've been longing for. First Corinthians 6:19-20 (NKJV) tells us *"Or do you not know that your body is the temple of the Holy Spirit who is in you, whom you have from God, and you are not your own? For you were bought at a price; therefore, glorify God in your body and in spirit, which are God's."* Since our bodies are literally God's sacred dwelling place, we have to be vigilant about what we put into our bodies both spiritually and physically. Tea for Two is designed to feed you spiritually and to give you natural remedies to everyday health issues. I used to be the queen of popping pain medication whenever I had a headache. Now I try to use natural remedies, such as drinking a cup of Mint tea when I have a headache.

It is my hope and prayer that you encounter the Lord like never before. I pray that during your daily devotions that you begin to experience incredible spiritual and physical healing. I pray that God allows your ears to be opened and your heart to receive all that He has in store for you over the next 30 days.

Day 1

TUNNEL VISION

Matthew 14:22-33

This evening while reading my nightly devotional, Jesus ministered to me from Matthew 14:22-33. He showed me that we can't have faith if we take our eyes off of Him and focus on what is happening in the natural. We must have tunnel vision with our eyes locked on Him.

Peter took his eyes off of Jesus, which had a negative effect on his faith. Peter's faith was strong while his eyes were locked on Jesus, but as soon as he looked away from Jesus and looked at the raging storm he was engulfed in, his faith diminished and he began to sink. When our faith begins to weaken, the pressures of life begin to overwhelm us and take us under.

How can we trust Jesus for a loved one's healing if we are fixated on the doctor's report? How can we trust Jesus for a promotion on our jobs if we focus on the skills we lack? It is impossible to have faith if we set our attention on everything and everyone but Jesus. Jesus is the Author and Finisher of our faith (Hebrews 12:2), which means that only by locking our eyes on Him can our faith flourish.

Faith also requires us to trust Jesus to do the impossible. When Peter stepped out of the boat, he fixed his eyes on Jesus and trusted Jesus to keep him above water. The Bible doesn't say that the storm ceased just because Jesus arrived near the boat. The storm was in full motion, but because Peter kept his eyes on Jesus, the storm became no more than background noise. When we're trusting Jesus to do the impossible, we have to tune out everything that contradicts our faith and we have to give Jesus our undivided attention. That means that we can't have one eye on Jesus and one eye on our circumstances. When we try to split our attention between Jesus and our circumstances, we become so enamored by the severity of our situation that we turn from Jesus to our situation and we begin to sink.

It is easy for us to become overwhelmed by our circumstances and forget that Jesus is within arm's reach waiting to help us. We must fix our eyes on Him so that our faith will be strengthened, and He can begin to do the impossible in our lives.

Prayer

Lord, help me to fix my eyes on You instead of my situation. You are the only One that can bring about change in my circumstances, so instead of focusing on my circumstances, help me to focus on You and Your faithfulness to me. You will not allow me to sink under the pressures of life, you will keep me afloat.

What's the Tea?

Chrysanthemum Tea

Have you ever had one of those days where you are struggling to focus at work? You have a million tasks to complete in a short span of time, but can't seem to even focus on one task. Maybe there are too many distractions in your office. Or maybe you can't stop thinking about your delicious leftovers from the night before that you have sitting in the refrigerator for lunch. If this has ever been you, what you needed in those moments was a good cup of alertness. One tea that can help you increase your mental focus and alertness is Chrysanthemum tea. Chrysanthemum tea is caffeine free, which will keep you from feeling jittery or experiencing the crash and burn that follows a caffeine high.

Flavor Profile:

Chrysanthemum tea is an herbal tea made from the Chrysanthemum (*Chrysanthemum indicum*) flower. The entire flower is steeped in hot water to make Chrysanthemum tea. Chrysanthemum tea is believed to have its origins in the Chinese Song Dynasty. This tea has a refreshing taste, a naturally sweet flavor, and a light, floral aroma.

Other Health Benefits:

In addition to increasing mental focus and alertness, Chrysanthemum tea can help cool the body naturally when experiencing a fever or heat stroke. Chrysanthemum tea can treat sore throats and pain caused by headaches and toothaches. This tea also contains much needed vitamins and minerals. Chrysanthemum tea is rich in Vitamins A, B, and C, and is packed with magnesium and calcium.

Other Teas to Try:

Other teas that can boost mental focus and increase alertness include:

❖ Green tea

❖ Black tea

❖ Oolong tea

❖ Ginkgo Biloba tea

Day 2

YOUR THOUGHTS TOWARDS OTHERS

Philippians 4:8

Have you ever noticed that when someone close to you has hurt you and you think about the situation, you become even angrier? It's like you're mentally reliving what they said or did and you feel the pain all over again.

I have always known that our thoughts influence us tremendously, but I have never thought about it in terms of how it impacts our relationships. Whenever I have applied *Philippians 4:8* to my life, I have always thought of it in terms of not thinking lustful thoughts, not doubting God when trusting Him, or being heavenly minded instead of letting my flesh rule my mind. I have never thought about thinking "lovely" thoughts towards someone who angered me. I knew that I had to eventually forgive that person and move forward from the situation, but to think good thoughts towards that person after they offended me hadn't crossed my mind.

It never occurred to me that the more I thought about the hurt that person inflicted, the more upset and frustrated I became with them and the more that hurt grew in my heart. What we think greatly influences our mood and attitudes (*Proverbs 15:13*). If we are thinking negatively about someone and what they did to us, we are not likely to be kind towards them. More than that, we will have a nasty attitude, which can cause division in other relationships. Are we really going to let what one person did cause problems in all our other relationships?

Instead of letting those negative thoughts towards someone continue, we need to bring the situation and that person before God. One of the most amazing things about God is that we can pour our hearts out to Him and He will not think differently of us. We can be brutally honest with Him about how we feel about that person who hurt us and He will love us just the same. Not only will we feel better afterwards, but we can also rest in God instead of dwelling on negative thoughts since we gave the situation to Him. He will also lead and guide us in the best way to handle the situation.

Prayer

Jesus, soften my heart towards those that have hurt and mistreated me. Keep me from thinking negatively about them, but instead help me to think loving thoughts about them. Let me pour my heart out to You about the injustice done to me instead of harboring it in my heart and mind.

What's the Tea?

Lavender Tea

Stress is an all too familiar feeling for many of us. Trying to find a healthy balance between work, relationships, and self-care can be overwhelming at times. I don't know about you, but I feel like I never have enough time to do anything. The days seem to fly by far too quickly, which adds to my stress. There are many ways to relieve stress. Some of my favorite stress relievers are journaling, exercising, or curling up with a good book and a hot cup of Lavender tea. Lavender tea can be used to help relieve stress and soothe your nerves. This tea has calming effects that can help relax the body and mind.

Flavor Profile:

Lavender tea is a floral tea that is made by brewing fresh or dried petals of the lavender flower (*Lavandula angustifolia*). Given that it is a floral tea, it has a soothing flowery aroma that can help bring a sense of tranquility. Some blends of Lavender tea have a light and semi-sweet flavor while others have a smoky flavor.

Other Health Benefits:

Individuals who struggle with anxiety and depression may benefit from drinking Lavender tea. Lavender tea has calming effects that can help those who suffer from insomnia. Lavender tea can also aid in alleviating digestive issues, such as stomachaches and indigestion.

Other Teas to Try:

Other teas that have a calming effect and reduce stress are:

❖ Mint tea

❖ Tulsi tea

❖ Oolong tea

❖ Black tea

Day 3

THE COMPARISON GAME

Hebrews 13:5

Do you play the comparison game? You know, that game where you examine your life in relation to others' lives? I've been guilty of playing this game. I would see my friends start new relationships, become engaged, or get married, and at first, I would be genuinely happy for them. However, I would start examining my own life in relation to theirs and ask myself, "What am I doing wrong? Why am I still single?" Asking myself those questions caused me to focus on my singleness instead of keeping my eyes on Christ, which led to dissatisfaction with my portion.

When we compare our lives to others', we are coveting what they have. We are so focused on what they have and what we don't have in comparison to them that we become unsatisfied with our portion. We will begin to believe the lie that until we get what is equivalent to their blessings, we won't be satisfied.

In *Hebrews 13:5* we are told not only to refrain from coveting what others have, but to also be satisfied with our own portion. My favorite part of this scripture is the reminder that Jesus will *never* leave us nor forsake us. Jesus is our ultimate portion. Nothing we receive in this life can compare to what we have in Jesus. All that other stuff, such as relationships, friendships, jobs, etc. are just extra blessings. *Jesus is our portion.* Once we fully grasp that all we need is Jesus and we keep that thought at the forefront of our minds, we won't get caught up in playing the comparison game.

Anytime we feel ourselves comparing our lives to others' lives, that means we have taken our eyes off of Jesus, and we have let discontentment into our hearts. When that starts to happen, immediately we need to get on our face before Jesus and pour our hearts out to Him. He knows the desires of our heart and He is the only one that can fulfill those desires. We also must remember that every season must come to an end. If we are miserable in our current season, moving to the next season will not take away that misery. Our hearts need to be changed first. We must first learn to be content with Jesus alone because He is the only One that can make us whole.

Prayer

Jesus, remove any jealousy or covetousness from my heart. Allow me to be content with my current season and with all that You have blessed me with. Keep me from engaging in the comparison game. Help me to be content with You, my greatest Portion and Gift.

What's the Tea?

Rooibos Tea

Trying to find the perfect skin care regimen can be difficult at times, especially if you have acne prone skin. There are numerous product lines to choose from that promise to give you beautiful, glowing skin. In any skin care regimen, what you put in your body is just as important as what you put on your face. One tea that can help fight acne is Rooibos tea. Rooibos tea is full of alpha hydroxy acid and zinc, which have both been shown to work wonders for the skin. Alpha hydroxy and zinc can help clear up acne, relieve eczema, heal sunburns, and reduce blemishes that cause uneven skin tone.

Flavor Profile:

Rooibos tea is an herbal tea that originates from the *Aspalathus linearis* bush in South Africa. This tea has a sweet yet earthy flavor. Its smoky flavor is complimented by a hint of sweet vanilla. Rooibos tea is also caffeine free, and, because of its sweet flavor, it does not require milk and sugar; however, if milk and sugar are added, only small amounts of each are needed.

Other Health Benefits:

In addition to aiding in skin care, Rooibos tea can also help relieve headaches, prevent insomnia, and treat allergies. Rooibos tea contains antioxidants including polyphenols, aspalathin, and nothofagin, which can strengthen one's immune system and fight against harmful diseases.

Other Teas to Try:

Other teas that can be used to treat certain skin conditions are:

- ❖ Calendula tea
- ❖ Oolong tea
- ❖ Green tea
- ❖ White tea

Day 4

FORGIVENESS. IS IT NECESSARY?

Ephesians 4:32

*F*orgiveness. A simple word, yet such a challenge for most of us to live out. When someone hurts us, the furthest thing from our mind is forgiving him or her. We're focused on the fact that someone wronged us and how horrible we feel. But once those emotions subside, what is our next move? Should we forgive or hold a grudge?

I have much experience with learning to forgive. From having a man hurt me in one of the worst ways possible to being rejected and mistreated by those I loved most, I have had to learn to forgive over the years. In the beginning, I opted not to forgive. I would try to rationalize with God, saying things like, *"But Lord, he hurt me in the worst possible way. I can't forgive him for that. He doesn't deserve my forgiveness!"* Every time I spoke those words,

God would respond, *"But beloved, I have forgiven you."* God's reason for responding to me this way was so that I could be like Him. As Christians, we are called to be like Christ.

When we refuse to forgive others for hurting us, we behave less like Christ and we open up a door for the enemy to come into our lives. The enemy will take that unforgiveness in our hearts and will have a field day with it. What's even worse is that he will make us blind to the consequences of our decision to hold onto unforgiveness. This is why God tells us to forgive.

Forgiveness isn't just for the person that hurt you. It's mostly for you in that it's the first step in setting you free from your past hurts. God can't begin to heal you of what that person has done to you until you take the first step by forgiving them. Also, when we don't forgive, God can't forgive us (*Matthew 6:15*). We must be like Christ and forgive so that we can receive that same forgiveness we so desperately need.

After living a life of withholding forgiveness, I truly believe that forgiveness is necessary for each of us. We must walk in forgiveness in order to avoid becoming bitter, miserable people and so that we can grow into the women and men God has called us to be.

Prayer

Jesus, search my heart and show me if there is anyone I have yet to forgive. Help me to walk in forgiveness towards them. Heal my hurting heart of the pain that they have inflicted on me. Give me clarity and guidance on how to live a life of forgiveness. Help me to also see that person through Your eyes instead of through my pain-filled eyes.

What's the Tea?

Cinnamon Tea

Approximately 5 million people around the world have been diagnosed with lupus. Each year there are approximately 16,000 new cases of lupus reported. Lupus is an autoimmune disease in which the immune system attacks the body's tissue and organs. This can lead to inflammation that negatively impacts the body's systems including the skin, joints, kidneys, brain, heart, blood cells, and lungs. When I was twelve years old, I was diagnosed with lupus. One of the symptoms I would often experience in the beginning was joint pain and swelling. For those who suffer from joint pain or swelling due to lupus, arthritis, or an injury, one tea that can help relieve these symptoms is Cinnamon tea. Cinnamon tea can relieve pain and swelling associated with inflammatory diseases.

Flavor Profile:

Cinnamon tea is native to Sri Lanka, southern India, Southeast Asia, and the West Indies. Cinnamon tea is an herbal tea that is made by brewing cinnamon

(*Cinnamomum*) bark. In addition to brewing crushed cinnamon bark in tea bags, Cinnamon tea can also be made by brewing cinnamon powder or cinnamon extract. This tea is aromatic and has a flavor that is a mixture of sweet honey and spice.

Other Health Benefits:

In addition to aiding in inflammatory conditions, Cinnamon tea can boost the immune system because of its antiviral, antifungal, and antibacterial properties. Cinnamon tea is also filled with antioxidants, which can help decrease the chance of strokes, heart attacks, and diabetes.

Other Teas to Try:

Other teas associated with relieving inflammation and joint pain include:

- ❖ Fennel tea
- ❖ Rosehip tea
- ❖ Moringa tea
- ❖ Pineapple tea
- ❖ Nettle tea

Day 5

BE STILL

Psalm 37:7

Have you ever felt like you were on the verge of something great…on the verge of a breakthrough? Things in your life are going fairly smoothly, you are getting on your face before Jesus daily, Jesus is speaking great things into your life, and you can literally see little by little Jesus making moves and setting things up for His plans for you to come into fruition. And then all of sudden, Jesus is quiet. You call on Him, but you don't hear His voice…

I've been through this before. There was a time when I went on a fast, which took me deeper in my relationship with Jesus. Jesus even started giving me a glimpse into His plans for me. He didn't reveal everything, but what He did show me left me speechless. I even started seeing Him put certain things in motion. But then all of sudden He became silent. This caused me to become anxious. I started questioning myself, asking if I had done something wrong, if I had pulled away from Him without even realizing it. The Lord told me:

"Be still, beloved. I am right here with you. Right now it seems like I'm not doing anything, but I am doing many things in the spiritual realm that you cannot see in the natural. Right now I want you to focus on resting in Me and trusting Me even when it seems like nothing is happening. The key to you successfully fulfilling My plans for your life is your trust in Me and you keeping your eyes on Me. Once you take your eyes off of Me, everything around you will begin to fall apart. You need Me every step of the way along this journey."

Jesus tells us to be still because He sees the whole picture while we see only a small portion of it. There are things that He has to develop in us before He fully moves us into a position to fulfill His plans for us and bring Him glory. It is a challenge being still when God gives us a glimpse into all that He has in store for us. It's even more challenging when we feel like we're so close to those plans coming to fruition, but they are not happening soon enough. Although it may not make sense as to why the fulfillment of these plans is dragging, we must put our trust in God. We have to fix our eyes on Him and trust His perfect timing.

Prayer

Jesus, help me to rest in You as You begin to fulfill Your plans for my life. Help me to be still and trust Your perfect timing. I trust You, Lord, and I will wait on You.

What's the Tea?

Licorice Tea

Although I love when the weather finally starts to cool down in the winter, I do not like the congestion and sore throats that it brings. Congestion and sore throats can leave you feeling miserable. One natural remedy that can help alleviate those flu-like symptoms is Licorice tea. Licorice tea can help relieve respiratory problems as well as coughing and bronchitis.

Flavor Profile:

Licorice tea is an herbal tea that is derived from the root of the licorice (*Glycyrrhiza glabra*) plant that is native to southeast Europe and southwest Asia. It is a sweet tea that is about 30 to 50 times sweeter than sugar. However, it does have a tart or tangy aftertaste.

Other Health Benefits:

Licorice tea can help decrease heartburn and relieve muscle cramps. It can also help improve certain digestive issues, such as stomach ulcers and irritable bowel syndrome.

Other Teas to Try:

Some other teas that can help relieve congestion or other respiratory issues are:

- ❖ Fennel tea

- ❖ Red Clover tea

- ❖ Chrysanthemum tea

- ❖ Peppermint tea

Day 6

PEACE THAT SURPASSES ALL UNDERSTANDING

Philippians 4:6-7 (NKJV)

When I first came to Christ, I would often hear *Philippians 4:7*. I would even meditate on it time and time again, but I never fully understood what the peace that surpasses all understanding meant or even how to access it. Ever since I was a child, I was a worrier. I would worry about everything. I would worry about things that children shouldn't even be concerned about, such as finances and having food on the table. Not to go into too much detail, but growing up things were hard for my mom and me. A lot of things that happened in my life were out of my control, which caused me to worry. This habit of worry followed me into adulthood even after I became a Christian.

I knew that God would give me a peace that surpasses all understanding, but I didn't know *how* to tap into that peace. *Philippians 4:6* tells us to be anxious for nothing, which is how we access God's peace. My mistake was that even after praying about a situation, I was still anxious about it. I was trying to figure everything out in the natural, but God doesn't work that way. Just because we can't see our prayer manifested in the natural does not mean that God is not working on our behalf. God is always working on our behalf.

I finally comprehend what the peace that surpasses all understanding is. It's a peace that remains with us in the midst of a crisis, a peace that sustains us in the midst of our life falling apart, a peace that allows us to keep it together in the midst of chaos. When we struggle with trusting God and tapping into His peace that surpasses all understanding, we must give those worries and concerns to Him. Any time worry starts to creep in our mind, we need to cast those thoughts down and start thanking God for what we are trusting Him for. We should praise Him as if that prayer has been manifested in the natural. As we continue to do this, it will become a habit and we will constantly have that peace that surpasses all understanding.

Prayer

Jesus, help me to cast all of my anxious thoughts onto You. Let me grab ahold of Your peace that surpasses all understanding instead of holding onto worry and fear. Allow me to rest in You confidently, knowing that You will work all things out for my good even when it doesn't look like it in the natural.

What's the Tea?

Honeybush Tea

Some nights it is such a battle to fall asleep. I toss and turn for hours without a wink of sleep in sight. I don't know if it is because I have too much on my mind or my body is simply being difficult. What I do know is that nights like that I wish I had something to make me pass out. One tea that can help with sleep troubles is Honeybush tea. Honeybush tea has calming effects, which will help you relax and get a good night's sleep.

Flavor Profile:

Honeybush tea is produced from the honeybush (*Cyclopia intermedia*) plant, which is native to certain parts of South Africa. The flavor of Honeybush tea is comparable to that of Rooibos tea; however, Honeybush tea is slightly sweeter than Rooibos tea and has a floral flavor.

Other Health Benefits:

Honeybush tea contains many antioxidants, which can

protect and strengthen the immune system. Another health benefit of Honeybush tea is that it can mimic estrogen in the body due to its phytoestrogenic properties, which is beneficial to menopausal women by helping to relieve menopause symptoms.

Other Teas to Try:

Other teas that can produce sleep-inducing effects are:

- ❖ Chamomile tea

- ❖ Lavender tea

- ❖ Lemon Balm tea

- ❖ Licorice tea

Day 7

GOD OPPORTUNITIES

Acts 1:16-21

This morning God ministered to me while reading Acts 1:16-21:

"I present each of My children with great opportunities. In Judas' case, it was to be one of Jesus' disciples and to help spread the Gospel. When I bring My children these opportunities, they have a choice: to accept it or reject it. If they choose to accept, that means they have to do it My way. It also means that they are going into this with blind trust because I will not reveal every detail of how it will happen. They have to trust that no matter what problems may arise or what sacrifices they have to make; I will work it all out in their favor. Accepting these opportunities leads to fulfillment and great blessings.

However, if My children reject My opportunities, I will find someone else with a willing heart to replace them, which is what happened to Judas. Also, when they reject these opportunities,

35

they are more vulnerable to becoming like the world. Their rejection of My opportunities leads to their choosing the world's opportunities, which will end in disaster and feelings of regret."

I have made the mistake of rejecting God opportunities. I let fear of the unknown, opposition from others, or belief that what the world has to offer is greater to cause me to reject opportunities from God. Judas made this same mistake by taking his eyes off of God and believing that what the world had to offer was better, which ended with him feeling tremendous regret and experiencing ample consequences.

When God presents us with an opportunity to glorify Him, we have a choice to make. We can bring Him glory by accepting the opportunity and trusting Him despite not knowing what all it will entail, or we can reject Him and miss out. We can't let uncertainty cause us to forfeit fulfilling God's marvelous plans for us. We may not fully understand the opportunity when God first presents it to us, but we can be confident that it will bring Him glory.

Prayer

Heavenly Father, when You present me with opportunities, help me to accept them with great joy. Keep fear or worry from causing me to miss out on the opportunity of a lifetime. Help me to trust You no matter what. I know You only want what's best for me.

What's the Tea?

White Mulberry Tea

Losing weight can be one of the most challenging and frustrating tasks. From trying to decide on which meal plan to follow to developing an exercise regimen, trying to lose weight can leave you feeling defeated. White Mulberry tea can help you on your weight loss journey. White Mulberry tea contains deoxy nojirimycin, which is a compound that can prevent the body from absorbing carbohydrates. Although carbohydrates provide our bodies with energy, if they are absorbed too quickly, it can lead to weight gain.

Flavor Profile:

White Mulberry tea is an herbal tea derived from the White Mulberry (*Morus alba*) tree, which is native to eastern and central China. Brewing dried or fresh leaves of the White Mulberry tree is how White Mulberry tea is made. White Mulberry tea has a light fragrance. This tea is smooth and slightly sweet similar to Green tea.

Other Health Benefits:

White Mulberry tea can help also lower cholesterol and blood glucose levels. Mulberry leaves contain calcium, zinc, and iron, making it a good source of minerals. It contains the antioxidant beta-carotene, which can help reduce the risk of cancer. Lastly, it has anti-inflammatory properties.

Other Teas to Try:

Other teas that can aid in weight loss are:

- ❖ Green tea
- ❖ White tea
- ❖ Vanilla tea
- ❖ Ginger tea

Day 8

BUT WHAT ABOUT
ME LORD?

Jeremiah 45

Jeremiah 45 is a message to Baruch, who was Jeremiah's scribe. During this time, Jeremiah was a very unpopular prophet (the people of Israel wanted to kill him because they did not like God's messages that he delivered to them), which also meant that the people of Israel disliked Baruch.

Baruch's words resonated with me so much (*Jeremiah 45:3*)! I have felt like this at different points in my life. At times things will continuously go wrong in my life, and it seems like as soon as I start to recover from the last blow, I'm struck with another one. At times it would get to the point where I would cry out to God saying, "Lord, when do I get a break?" It can be so discouraging at times! One time when I was feeling defeated, God began to minister to me through this scripture. He told me,

"Just like Baruch began to take his eyes off of Me, you are doing the same thing. Fix your eyes on Me. It's not about you. It's not about what you can get or what you think you deserve. It's about serving Me and glorifying Me. I know that you are tired; I know that you want a break, but this is for My glory. Keep your eyes on Me, keep serving Me, and remember that you have others watching you. Your life is a testimony. How you live your life allows others to see Me. Remember that and I will strengthen you. I will give you rest, but you have to keep your eyes on Me."

God's words to me seriously convicted me. I forgot that this life is not meant to be comfortable. This life isn't meant to be easy, but I must remember, *"for our present troubles are small and won't last very long. Yet they produce for us a glory that vastly outweighs them and will last forever"* (*2 Corinthians 4:17, NLT*). God has great purpose for our suffering. Even though it hurts, even though it is discouraging, even though it feels like it is unfair, we have to remember Who we are living this life for. Are we living this life for our own enjoyment and comfort? Or are we living this life for Christ? We are enduring these trials to glorify Christ. It's not about us, it's about Him.

Prayer

Jesus, help me to remember that this life is not about me, but about You and You alone. When I suffer, help me to pick up my cross, endure the pain, and remember that You are with me every step of the way and that You will strengthen and encourage me.

What's the Tea?

Linden Tea

Whenever I have a long day at work, I tend to go home with a nagging headache. I could just pop a pain-killer, but then I think about the damage that is done internally every time I take one, which often deters me. I try massaging my temples, but that only seems to relieve the pain temporarily. A natural remedy that can help relieve that horrible pounding in your head is Linden tea.

Flavor Profile:

Linden tea is made from the bark, leaves, or flowers of the summer linden (*Tilia platyphyllos*) tree or the winter linden (*Tilia cordata*) tree. Linden trees are native to North America and Europe. These trees are known by various names including basswood, lime tree, lime flower, and silver lime. Linden tea has a semi-sweet flavor and a floral scent, which is attributed to the oils found in the linden flowers.

Other Health Benefits:

Linden tea can help cure flu-like symptoms, such as fevers and sore throats. It can also bring relief to ear infections, stomach indigestion, and itchy skin.

Other Teas to Try:

Other teas that can aid in relieving headaches include:

- ❖ Rooibos tea

- ❖ Lavender tea

- ❖ Peppermint tea

- ❖ Rosemary tea

Day 9

THE POWER OF
OUR WORDS

Luke 6:6-10

Have you ever had someone say something negative to you and it literally ruins your entire mood? It's like that one statement zapped all of the joy and happiness out of you.

Our words hold so much power, yet too often we use them carelessly. At times we speak out of anger, insecurities, or simply speak without thinking. In those moments we can cause so much destruction. It's during those moments that we fail to use our words the way that God intended.

I believe that God intended for us to use our words to bring life and healing. In today's reading, we read about how Jesus healed the man with the deformed hand. Unlike many of His other healings and miracles,

Jesus did not lay His hands on this man. Jesus simply told the man to stretch out his hand and then the man's hand was healed. This scripture provides an example of what we are to do with our words.

Our words are supposed to encourage and bring healing. We are foolish when we make little snide, sarcastic, or rude comments, and wise when we speak loving, kind words (*Proverbs 12:18*). Our words can either be sweet like honey or bitter like poison (*Proverbs 16:24*). Since negative words are like poison, they have harmful effects. Not only do our negative words harm those we say them to, but they also poison our minds and hearts.

We are to glorify God with our words by uplifting others. Our words should line up with what God's Word says. If it contradicts God's Word, then we shouldn't be speaking it. Speak life instead of death and bring about healing like Jesus did with His words. Give someone an encouraging word today!

Prayer

Jesus, thank You for providing the perfect example of someone who speaks life. Help me to glorify You with my words. Lord, teach me to speak life to everyone I encounter. Allow my words to be sweet like honey and uplift everyone I speak to. Help me to think before I speak

and make sure that my words never contradict Your
Word.

What's the Tea?

Rose Tea

Looking for a natural way to increase your Vitamin C intake? Although taking a Vitamin C capsule is quick, it is not always easy, especially for those who have a hard time swallowing pill. Try a cup of Rose tea, which is high in Vitamin C. Drinking a cup of tea is much easier to ingest than swallowing a capsule. Also, consuming vitamins from food sources is easier for the body to absorb than taking vitamins in pill form.

Flavor Profile:

Roses are believed to have originated from Persia. The rose plant is native to Europe and North Africa. Rose tea is made by brewing either fresh or dried rose petals from the rose (*Rosa rugosa*) plant. This tea has a slightly sweet, fruity flavor and a floral scent, making it a delicious alternative to taking capsules to get your daily Vitamin C intake.

Other Health Benefits:

The Vitamin C in Rose tea brings other health benefits including helping boost the immune system and assisting in collagen production, which creates healthy skin and hair. Rose tea can also aid women in relieving menstrual cramps as well as a few other symptoms associated with the menstrual cycle.

Other Teas to Try:

Other teas rich in Vitamin C are:

- ❖ Black Currant tea
- ❖ White Pine tea
- ❖ Saffron tea
- ❖ Thyme tea

Day 10

DOES GOD CARE ABOUT THE SMALL STUFF?

Luke 12:6-7

Have you ever had a day where everything seemed to be going wrong? You woke up late for work and then in a rush you forgot your lunch at home. Then at the end of your workday you come outside to find that you have a flat tire. These situations are a pain, but they are minor. Have you ever wondered if God cares about those minor incidents in your life?

God cares about every aspect of our life, both big and small. Sure, we can easily go and fix the small stuff, but He wants us to bring those situations to Him and pour our hearts out to Him. Although those problems are minor, they are still frustrating and can cause our attitude to turn for the worse. That's why we bring those problems to Him.

In my experience, pouring my heart out to God about the small stuff gives me so much peace and joy. It's such an incredible feeling knowing that my Lord and Savior cares about the small upsets that occurs in my life and listens to me when I talk to Him about those issues.

I think sometimes we as Christians underestimate how much God cares about what happens in our lives. We tend to limit Him with our thinking. We think that He has more important matters to deal with than to care about our insignificant issues. We have to change that thinking. Based on today's scripture, how can we say that God doesn't care about every aspect of our life? He made it a point to know the number of hairs on our head! I don't even know how many hairs are on my head nor have I tried to find out, but God took the time to know. That's how much He cares about us! He wants to know *every single detail of our lives!*

We can truly talk to God about anything. He has the greatest solution to even the smallest of problems. He will cover us with His peace and joy, which will make the situation so much easier to handle. He understands the frustrations of everyday life. He is such a loving and caring God. We just have to open up to Him.

Prayer

Heavenly Father, thank You for loving me so much and taking the time to know me better than anyone else. The fact that someone as mighty as You took the time to know the very number of hairs on my head makes me feel so loved. Help me to never forget Your unfailing love for me and to bring every issue, big or small, to You.

What's the Tea?

Ginger Tea

Made the decision to get back into the gym and now your muscles are sore to the point that you can barely move? Or maybe you've decided to push yourself even harder in the gym, but now your muscles are yelling at you in protest? Whatever the case may be, Ginger tea may be the answer to your fatigued muscles! Ginger tea contains properties that help prevent inflammation, which can aid in relieving muscle soreness.

Flavor Profile:

Ginger tea is made from the underground root of the ginger root (*Zingiber officinale*) plant, which is native to China. Ginger tea is an herbal tea that has an intense warm and spicy flavor, and a powerful aroma. Ginger tea's warm and spicy flavor also warms your body from head to toe. To help cut the intense flavor of this tea, add 1-2 tablespoons of honey.

Other Health Benefits:

Ginger tea can help relieve nausea, increase blood flow to cleanse the body of toxins, decrease cholesterol, prevent the blood from clotting, and increase metabolism to promote weight loss.

Other Teas to Try:

Other teas that can help relieve muscle tension are:

- ❖ Chamomile tea

- ❖ Marshmallow tea

- ❖ Wild Yam tea

- ❖ Hyssop tea

Day 11

HOW DO YOU
HANDLE CRITICISM?

Proverbs 27:5

Whenever I hear the word criticism, I cringe. I have always thought of that word in a negative sense. Whenever I feel like someone is criticizing me, I often get on the defensive and become downright angry.

The Lord led me to read *Proverbs 27:5* during my quiet time with Him one day. He then began to minister to me about how I react to my mom when she lovingly corrects me. I literally shut down on her and, in my head, I feel like she's being mean and judgmental. He showed me that she's not trying to hurt me or belittle me, but that she's trying to help me grow into the woman God has called me to be.

God further ministered to me about this topic through *Proverbs 29:1 (NLT)*, "*Whoever stubbornly refuses to accept criticism will suddenly be destroyed beyond recovery."* Destroyed beyond recovery? Those words terrify me! Basically, when we refuse to listen to someone who is correcting us, we end up making mistakes. If we continue to reject those who are correcting us, eventually we will make a mistake that will ultimately lead to our downfall, preventing us from recovering from it.

I thank God for not allowing that to happen, but I know if I continue to refuse to accept criticism or respond in anger when I am being lovingly corrected, His mercy will run out. We need those in our life who are going to correct us when we are wrong, those who are not going to sugarcoat things, but tell it like it is. I'm not talking about those who are really trying to discourage us or find fault with everything we do. I'm talking about those who truly love us and, because they have our best interest at heart, they are going to tell us what we need to hear no matter how difficult it may be.

We need to learn how to humbly receive criticism, take it before the Lord, and allow Him to correct and transform us. It will be painful, but it will be so worth it in the end. As we continue to accept criticism, we will grow into the person God has called us to be.

Prayer

Lord, humble me so that I willingly accept the loving criticism of those who want what's best for me. Remove that prideful spirit from me and allow me to receive their criticism gladly. I know that You will use this criticism to shape me into the person You created me to be and to make me like You.

What's the Tea?

Horsetail Tea

Many of us dream of having longer hair and stronger nails. There are many vitamins and supplements on the market that claim to promote nail and hair growth. If you're not a fan of taking pills, especially those the size of horse pills, there is a much easier option. Horsetail tea contains high levels of silica, which promotes hair and nail growth.

Flavor Profile:

Horsetail tea is brewed from the Horsetail (*Equisetum arvense*) plant, which is a perennial herb that is native to Asia, Europe, and North America. The Horsetail plant has grass-like sheaths that grow out of the main stem of the plant, which are brewed to make Horsetail tea. This herbal tea has a light aroma and flavor.

Other Health Benefits:

In addition to promoting hair and nail growth, Horsetail

tea can be used to prevent bloating, strengthen bones, and heal fungal infections. It can be used to stop bleeding and heal internal wounds, such as ulcers that are bleeding, hemorrhoids, and heavy periods. The silica found in Horsetail tea promotes healthy lung tissue and helps repair damaged lung tissue. Horsetail tea provides many benefits to the urinary tract. Specifically, Horsetail tea can reduce inflammation in the urinary tract, rid the body of urinary tract infections, and act as a mild diuretic to remove toxins from the body.

Other Teas to Try:

Other teas that contain high levels of silica to promote hair and nail growth are:

❖ Bamboo Leaf tea

❖ Oat Straw tea

❖ Nettles tea

Day 12

A SEASON OF
RELENTLESS STORMS

Isaiah 48:10

Have you ever been in a season where you were being bombarded by attacks from the enemy? As soon as you try to recover from one attack, another one occurs. There's no rest from these attacks, you're getting hit from the left and the right. You're crying out to God, but there's still no relief. You feel as if He's forgotten about you, as if this season of storms will never end. You can't help but wonder why…what did you do to deserve this? It's to the point that you've cried so much that you wonder if you even have any tears left. You're not sure how much more you can take before you break.

During these seasons, God is developing and maturing us for what He has called us to do. These seasons are painful because God is refining us. This means that He is removing certain attitudes and behaviors, and anything that contradicts Him so that we can become like Him and fulfill His plans for our life.

Since God uses these relentless storms to refine us, we need to ask Him what characteristic He is trying to develop in us. When we begin to view these seasons of never-ending storms as a time of refinement, our perspective will change. Instead of wallowing in our sorrows and having a "woe is me" mindset, we will focus on the lessons God is teaching us. These lessons are valuable and will prepare us for the next season of our life.

When we're in a season of constant storms, it may feel like God has abandoned us, but He hasn't. His word says"...*He will never leave you nor forsake you*" (Deut. 31:6, NIV). Instead of letting these challenging seasons defeat us, we need to stand on this promise and have faith that He is with us even in the midst of these storms. When we start seeing these seasons as periods of growth instead of difficult times, we will make it through them with joy and looking more like Christ.

Prayer

Jesus, thank You for these seasons of relentless storms. Thank You for refining me so that I become more and more like You, and less like this world. Help me to always view these seasons as seasons of growth and development instead of trials and tribulations. Open my eyes so that I can see the character You are trying to build in me, and the attitudes and behaviors You are trying to uproot out of me. Help me to yield to Your hand instead of resisting the change in me You are bringing about.

What's the Tea?

Hibiscus Tea

Approximately 1 in 3 American adults have been diagnosed with prehypertension. Prehypertension is a condition in which an individual's blood pressure counts are higher than normal, but not high enough to be considered high blood pressure. A natural way to help manage prehypertension is by drinking Hibiscus tea. Research has shown that individuals who suffer from prehypertension may have a reduction in their blood pressure when they incorporate a cup of Hibiscus tea into their daily diet.

Flavor Profile:

Hibiscus tea is derived from the flowers of the *Hibiscus sabdariffa* plant, which are native to North Africa and Southeast Asia. Brewing the dried calyces of the hibiscus plant makes Hibiscus tea. The calyx of the hibiscus plant is the part of the plant that preserves and holds the hibiscus flower. Hibiscus tea has a tart flavor similar to cranberry juice. This tea is caffeine free and can be served either hot or iced.

Other Health Benefits:

Hibiscus tea has antioxidant properties that help lower cholesterol and protect the liver. Hibiscus tea has antibacterial properties, aids in digestion, and acts as a diuretic, which can help flush excess water from the body.

Other Teas to Try:

Other teas that can aid in reducing high blood pressure and help manage prehypertension are:

- ❖ Fennel tea
- ❖ Mulberry tea
- ❖ Ginger tea
- ❖ Ginseng tea
- ❖ Green tea

Day 13

SHUT THE FLESH UP!

Galatians 5:17

This verse makes me think about the continuous battle between our spirit and flesh, which is no joke. It is a constant struggle between our spirit, which wants to honor and obey God, and our flesh, which wants to indulge in selfish desires and do everything that is contrary to God's Word.

In order to be a true Christ follower, we are to indulge the spirit and neglect the flesh, which is easier said than done. Denying the flesh is painful. We are denying our flesh what it wants, and in turn our flesh responds like a two-year-old throwing a full-blown tantrum. I'm talking kicking, screaming, crying...the works!

Although denying our flesh is no easy task, it is worth it in the end. When we deny our flesh, we submit to God's law and we *please* God (*Romans 8:7-8*). It is such an amazing feeling to walk in obedience and please God.

What's even better is that we don't have to try to deny our flesh in our own ability.

Zechariah 2:13 tells us one of the ways to deny the flesh, which is by being in the Presence of the Lord. When we are in God's Presence, our flesh must be quiet because He is holy. You want to deny your flesh? Get on your face before God daily in His word, prayer and worship. The key word is *daily*. We have to deny our flesh 24/7 and it's not something we can do in our own willpower. If that were the case, Jesus wouldn't have had to die on the cross for our sins. By spending time with God, we will be in His Presence, which will silence our flesh. By silencing our flesh, it becomes weaker and our spirit becomes stronger. When our spirit is stronger than our flesh, we are better equipped to walk in holiness and obedience to God. Simply put, we have to shut the flesh up!

Prayer

Jesus, give me the strength to deny my flesh. Help me to honor You in all that I say and do. Develop in me a strong spirit of self-control so that I will deny my flesh and let my spirit man rule over my flesh. Create in me a hunger and thirst for Your Presence. If there is anything that is distracting me or preventing me from spending time in Your Presence, remove it from my life.

What's the Tea?

Rosehip Tea

Every day we come into contact with countless germs. There are a wide variety of disinfectants we can use and supplements we can take to protect ourselves from catching the flu and boost our immune system. A healthy and natural way to boost our immune system is by drinking Rosehip tea. Rosehip tea is high in both vitamins A and C. Vitamin A strengthens our immune system by clearing out toxins; vitamin C fights against bacterial and viral infections. By drinking 3-4 cups of Rosehip tea a day, you can reduce your chances of catching the flu.

Flavor Profile:

Rosehip tea is made by brewing the small, red fruit from the rose (*Rosaru gosa*) plant. Rosehips form once the petals of the rose fall off. The rosehips are the part of the plan that contain the highest amounts of vitamin C. Similar to Hibiscus tea, Rosehip tea has a tangy, semi-sweet flavor.

Other Health Benefits:

Rosehip tea is rich in antioxidants, which help prevent certain diseases such as heart disease, arthritis, and cancer. Rosehip tea acts as an antidepressant, helps relieve stress, strengthens and energizes the kidneys, and treats urinary tract infections.

Other Teas to Try:

Other teas that help boost the immune system are:

- ❖ Green tea

- ❖ Chamomile tea

- ❖ Elderberry tea

- ❖ Lemongrass tea

Day 14

ANCHOR OF MY HOPE

Hebrews 6:19

Ever had one of those mornings where it did not start off the best? One of those days that started off with disappointments and unexpected changes? I have had plenty of days like this. One morning while I was talking to God about how my morning did not start off right and thanking Him for helping me to remain calm instead of reacting and letting my emotions rule me, God ministered to me:

"Beloved, just like when an anchor is dropped to keep a ship still and, in its place, it is the same way I keep you still and calm in the midst of a storm."

This is what Jesus does for us. Life is not perfect. Nine times out of ten something is going to go wrong. The unexpected will happen. People will disappoint us daily. Things will be lost, relationships broken, but in the midst of it all, Jesus is there to keep us grounded…to keep us from losing our minds. He overwhelms us with His love and peace...His joy...He is our Anchor of Hope.

According to Vine's Expository Dictionary of New Testament Words, the Greek word for hope is elpis, which means *"favorable and confident expectation."* In Hebrews 6:19, it refers to how hope is expressed "in endurance under trial." Jesus is the anchor of our hope in that we put our "favorable and confident expectation" in Him during trials, and by doing so we persevere through these trials.

I am so thankful that I have Jesus as my anchor of hope. I honestly could not make it in this life without Him keeping me grounded daily. Seriously, I would have lost my mind or been dead if it wasn't for Him.

When everything that can go wrong does go wrong, lean on your Anchor of Hope...allow Jesus to keep you grounded in the midst of your storm. Everything around us can be complete and utter chaos, but as long as we have our Anchor of Hope [Jesus], we will be calm and grounded in the midst of it all.

Prayer

Thank You Jesus for being my Anchor of Hope. Thank You for keeping me calm in the midst of chaos and confusion. Whenever I am overwhelmed by life, help me to remember to look to You with great expectation. You will never allow the trials that arise in my life to overtake me. I will rest in You and trust You to work all things out in my favor.

What's the Tea?

Moringa Tea

I don't know about you, but some days it is such a struggle to get through work without yawning or feeling fatigued. Some days it is such a struggle to do even the simplest tasks because I have no energy. On days like this, instead of reaching for a cup of coffee, try a cup of Moringa tea. Moringa tea is full of antioxidants and other compounds that keep the thyroid healthy, which increases and maintains high energy levels.

Flavor Profile:

Moringa tea is brewed from the dried leaves of the moringa (*Moringa oleifera*) plant. The moringa plant is native to India, Pakistan, and Nepal. Moringa tea has a plant-like flavor making the taste not so pleasant. However, adding honey can sweeten the flavor and allow you to get that energy boost you need to power through your day.

Other Health Benefits:

In addition to boosting your energy, Moringa tea is beneficial to those diagnosed with diabetes. This tea has been found to decrease blood sugar levels and cholesterol as well as increase protection against cell damage. Moringa tea also promotes brain health. It is rich in vitamins C and E, which are effective in preventing neurons from degenerating and improving overall brain function. It also balances certain hormones in the brain that influence memory, mood, how we respond to stress and pleasure, and mental health.

Other Teas to Try:

Other teas that also work as energy boosters are:

❖ Green tea

❖ Ginkgo Biloba tea

❖ Dong Quai tea

❖ Bitter Orange tea

Day 15

LOVING AS
CHRIST LOVES US

John 13:34

Jesus commands us to love others as He loves us. This is easier said than done. Just thinking about how much Jesus loves us…it's hard to wrap our minds around it. His love for us is unconditional; it has no limits or boundaries. He loves us with reckless abandon. Think about it: His ultimate act of love was dying on the cross for our sins so that we can spend eternity with Him. Not only did Jesus die for us, but He also died for us while we were *still* sinners (*Romans 5:8*). We didn't have to perfect ourselves or do anything to earn His love. He loved us just because. This is the kind of love He wants us to display to others.

Demonstrating this unconditional love is easy when dealing with those who are kind to us…but what about those who hate us or continue to hurt us? Do we *have* to love them too? Are we only supposed to be kind to those who treat us right? Or do we only do for those we know will give us something in return?

In *Luke 6:32-36* (*NKJV*) Jesus tells us that we are no different than the world if we simply love those who treat us right and do for us. If we look just like the world, how can we be the light of the world? Part of what makes us stand out as Christians is our love walk. When we are kind to those who use and abuse us, that's what makes people look at us and see that there is something different. That's loving as Christ does.

At times it is a challenge to love as Christ loves us, especially if we're having a bad day, don't feel well, or have to be kind to someone who hurt us. Despite all of that, we are still called to love others as Christ loves us. When we think about how much Jesus loves us and how we don't deserve His love, it makes it so much easier to love others unconditionally.

Prayer

Jesus, thank You for loving me unconditionally even though I don't deserve it. Teach me to love as You love. Give me a heart like Yours that loves unconditionally and loves those who mistreat You. Give me eyes like

Yours so that I can see people through Your love filled eyes.

What's the Tea?

Echinacea Tea

When I was a child, I used to always get ear infections. It felt like every week I had an ear infection. Ear infections are the worst. I would rather have a fever or a sore throat than endure an ear infection. One tea that may aid in clearing up an ear infection is Echinacea tea. Since Echinacea tea promotes the production of antibodies and interferon, which help block viral infections, this tea will help speed up the healing process of an ear infection. It is recommended that two grams of the Echinacea herb in the form of tea should be consumed three times a day for no more than 10 days in order to heal an ear infection.

Flavor Profile:

Echinacea tea is made by steeping in hot water the roots, stems, and flowers of the Black Samson Coneflower (*Echinacea angustifolia*) herb that is found in the Rocky Mountains and Great Plains region. Echinacea tea has a potent floral flavor and scent. Fresh lemon or citrusy herbs can be added to temper the flavor of the tea.

Other Health Benefits:

Echinacea tea is great for fighting the common cold as well as reducing the chances of catching a cold. It is helpful in relieving stomachaches, sore throats, and toothaches. When Echinacea tea is consumed on a daily basis, your immune system will be strengthened and your body will be able to easily ward off bacteria, fungus, and viruses.

Other Teas to Try:

Other teas that may help heal ear infections are:

- ❖ Chamomile tea

- ❖ Yarrow tea

- ❖ Angelica Root tea

Day 16

TAKING MATTERS INTO OUR OWN HANDS

1 Samuel 13:7-14

Have you ever prayed and asked God to help you make a decision about a certain matter, but it seemed like He was taking too long to respond? Maybe it was about whether or not to take a certain job or some other pressing matter? Did you wait on God for a response or did you make the decision without Him?

I have made the mistake of taking matters into my own hands plenty of times. I felt like God was taking too long to respond so I chose to make the decision independently. Like King Saul, I looked at what was happening in the natural instead of fixing my eyes on God, which led to me becoming anxious. When we are distracted by the state of our situation, we become impatient and we take matters into our own hands.

As we read in today's scripture, King Saul and the

Israelites were in the middle of a war against the Philistines. King Saul was instructed to wait seven days for Samuel to come to offer a sacrifice to God. Saul waited, but then he became anxious because his army was discouraged since Samuel had yet to arrive. This led Saul to take matters into his own hands and offer the sacrifice even though he knew it was against God's will.

When we take matters into our own hands, we are pretty much telling God, "I got this. I know what's best for me. I don't need Your guidance." We also step out of God's will for our lives since we are following our own plans. When we're no longer in God's will for our lives, our lives lead to disaster. Every move we make causes our lives to get worse and worse.

The reason why is that our human nature makes us selfish and flawed, which means that our plans and decisions are selfish and flawed. We see this in the life of King Saul. After he stepped out of God's will for his life, he made bad decision after bad decision. His life went downhill all because He was no longer in alignment with God.

In order to stay in God's will for our lives, we need to walk in obedience. There will be times when it seems like God is taking a while to answer our prayers. We can't let the waiting period cause us to panic. We must wait on Him and trust Him to show us what to do. Even if the situation appears to be getting worse, we must trust His perfect timing and wait for Him to show us what to do so that we can stay in alignment with His will. If we rest in Him and trust Him to work everything out in our favor, we won't let worry and fear cause us to do our will instead of His.

Prayer

Heavenly Father, help me to yield total control of my life to You. Lead me and guide me in everything I do. Develop patience in me so that I wait on You instead of taking matters into my own hands. Help me to keep my eyes on You instead of my circumstances.

What's the Tea?

Sage Tea

Have you ever been overwhelmed by anxiety? Maybe you're worried about a job you recently interviewed for or an upcoming doctor's appointment? In addition to praying and giving your worries and fears to Jesus, you can try a cup of Sage tea. Sage tea can reduce anxiety by improving your mood and promoting alertness and calmness.

Flavor Profile:

Sage tea is brewed from the leaves of the Sage (*Salvia officinalis*) plant, which is native to Southern Europe and the Mediterranean. Sage tea has a powerful pungent, bitter flavor. However, adding honey or simply brewing sage leaves with a sweet, herbal fruit tea can cut the bitterness of Sage tea and allow you to still reap its benefits.

Other Health Benefits:

In addition to producing calmness in the midst of feeling

anxious, Sage tea is rich in antioxidants. These antioxidants help prevent premature aging by stopping the free radicals from damaging the body's tissue and cells. Sage tea aids in reducing fevers, fighting colds, healing sore throats, and relieving headaches. Sage tea can help lower blood sugar levels and relieve indigestion and gas.

Other Teas to Try:

Other teas that also help reduce anxiety are:

- ❖ Damiana tea

- ❖ Honeybush tea

- ❖ Lavender tea

- ❖ Lemon Balm tea

- ❖ Vervain tea

Day 17

SAME BODY, DIFFERENT CALLINGS

Romans 12:4-5 (NLT)

This morning while reading my devotional, I began to think about how often I've felt as if my calling was insignificant in comparison to others' callings. I felt like I wasn't doing enough for the Kingdom. I also felt like my gifts and calling weren't making an important impact like other Christians.

At times we as Christians compare our callings to others' callings, which is one thing we should never do. No calling is greater than another. Yes, each calling and gift is different, but no one calling is greater than another, nor is one more important than another. Every calling is equal but different.

Today's reading shows us that each of us has a *special function*. It does not say that each of us has a better function or an insignificant function, nor does it tell us that one function is greater or lesser than another. According to *Vine's Complete Expository Dictionary of Old and New Testament Words,* the Hebrew word for special is *tuchōn,* which means "not common or ordinary." Since each of our callings is "not common or ordinary," that means that each of us has a calling that is unique, rare, and one of a kind. Our calling cannot be fulfilled by anyone but us. This shows that no calling is unimportant or insignificant. Every calling matters and is especially important within the body of Christ.

God created each of us with a special function in mind. Each of our callings has one common goal: to add to the Kingdom of Heaven. Whenever we feel like we aren't doing enough for the kingdom or our calling isn't making a difference to the Kingdom of Heaven, we need to remember that what we do is just as important as what someone else is doing for the Kingdom. Also, we need to stop comparing our calling to someone else's. That's how we stir up discontentment and jealousy. We should focus on being content with the portion God has given us.

Prayer

Heavenly Father, thank You for creating me to fulfill the calling You have given me. Thank You for choosing me to fulfill this purpose. Keep me from becoming discouraged or discontent with Your purpose for my life. Use me how You want to use me. Help me to remember that it's about adding to Your Kingdom and to know and believe that my calling is just as important as the next.

What's the Tea?

Red Clover Tea

Feeling worn out, bloated, or having trouble falling asleep at night? These could be signs that your body is in dire need of a detox. There are many detox drinks and diets on the market today, but one natural and inexpensive way of giving your body a much needed detox is drinking Red Clover tea. Red Clover tea works as a diuretic, causing one to urinate more, which leads to removing toxins and fat from the body.

Flavor Profile:

Red Clover tea is brewed from the leaves and flowers of the Red Clover (*Trifolium pretense*) herb. The Red Clover herb is native to Europe and Asia. Red Clover tea is sweet like candy causing it to not need sugar or honey added to it.

Other Health Benefits:

Red Clover tea aids in lowering cholesterol levels and

blood pressure. This tea is rich in Vitamin C and antioxidants, both of which strengthen the immune system. It can help relieve respiratory conditions including bronchitis, colds, and asthma.

Other Teas to Try:

Other teas that act as a diuretic are:

❖ Dandelion tea

❖ Horsetail tea

❖ Parsley tea

❖ Plantain tea

❖ Yarrow tea

Day 18

Awaiting a Response

Daniel 10:11-14 (NKJV)

Have you ever been praying and trusting God for something major in your life? Maybe it was for a promotion at your job, restoring your marriage, or a financial break-through so that you can get out of debt. What do you do when it seems like God isn't answering your prayers and the situation is getting worse? Do you feel like He's ignoring you or that maybe He isn't going to answer your prayers?

Daniel is someone who has firsthand experience with waiting on God to answer his prayers. Just to give some background on the story, Daniel had a vision about the end times and didn't understand what the vision meant (Daniel 10:1). Since he wanted God to give him wisdom and insight into this vision, he prayed and fasted (Daniel 10:2-3). As we can see in today's reading, 21 days went by and Daniel received no response from God, which was due to an evil spirit trying to prevent the manifestation of Daniel's answered prayer. God answered Daniel's prayer immediately, but the enemy and his demons were trying to prevent the angel from delivering God's response to Daniel.

Daniel is an excellent example of how we need to be when we are waiting on God for a response to our prayer. Not once while Daniel was waiting for God to answer his prayers did he begin to worry or become anxious. Instead he fasted and prayed. That's exactly how we need to be when we are waiting on God to answer our prayers. We shouldn't automatically assume the worst and think that God isn't going to answer our prayers. We need to rest in God knowing that He hears our prayers and will give us a response in His perfect timing.

Whenever we pray and are awaiting a response from God, we must remember that He hears our prayers, but there are things occurring in the spiritual realm that delay the manifestation of our answered prayers. The enemy doesn't want God to answer our prayers, which is why him and his demons try to prevent God's answers from reaching us. Instead of worrying or getting frustrated, we need to rest in God and trust Him to answer our prayers.

Prayer

Heavenly Father, help me to not worry or fret when waiting for You to answer my prayers. I know that the enemy tries to stop Your answers to my prayers from reaching me so that I will take my eyes off of You and no longer trust You. Help me to rest in You and know that You work all things out for my good.

What's the Tea?

Peach Tea

As we grow older, sometimes our vision begins to decline. It may become harder to see while driving at night or much more of a challenge to read the small print on our cell phones and computer screens. One way to prolong healthy vision and prevent blindness is by drinking Peach tea. Peach tea is rich in beta-carotene, which the body transforms into Vitamin A. Vitamin A strengthens the eyes and protects the eyes from various vision related diseases.

Flavor Profile:

Peach tea is an herbal tea brewed from leaves or the bark of the peach (*Prunus persica*) plant. Peach tea is often brewed with other teas, such as Black tea or White tea. Freshly brewed Peach tea produces a pleasant scent and has a sweet and fruity flavor.

Other Health Benefits:

Peach tea contains magnesium, which helps reduce stress and anxiety as well as calm the nervous system. Peach tea also lowers cholesterol and contains anti-aging properties.

Other Teas to Try:

Other teas that support eye health are:

- ❖ Moringa tea

- ❖ Saffron tea

- ❖ Bilberry tea

- ❖ Fennel tea

- ❖ Eyebright tea

Day 19

LIVING A LIFE
OF EXCELLENCE

Genesis 24:12-21 (NKJV)

How do you feel when you hire someone to do a job for you and they do it halfway? Maybe you hired someone to paint your living room and when they finished, it looked like a two-year old threw paint at your walls. How do you think God feels when we do a less than mediocre job as Christians? Maybe our love walk is more rude and critical than loving and kind. Maybe our quiet time with Him consists of us checking our phones every two minutes instead of giving Him our undivided attention. Is God pleased with us when we give Him less than our best?

As believers, we are called to a higher standard. We are to give God our very best in all that we do and we are to live a life of excellence. Rebekah is someone who gave God her very best. In this story, Abraham sends his servant to Abraham's home country to find a wife for his son Isaac. The servant sets out on a long journey with 10 camels carrying various gifts for the future Mrs. Isaac. When the servant arrives to Abraham's country, he stops at the well right outside the city. Him and his camels are dying of thirst. Since he's unsure of what to do next, he prays to God asking for guidance. As soon as he finishes praying, Rebekah arrives at the well. Rebekah had no clue as to who this man was or why he was at the well. Instead of questioning or giving him attitude when he asked her for a drink of water, she not only gave him water but she also drew water for his 10 camels.

What Rebekah did is an amazing example of living a life of excellence. She went over and beyond for a complete stranger! Now picture this: it's a scorching hot, sunny day and Rebekah is heading to the well to get water for her family. She goes down to the well to fill up a jug that can hold a gallon of water, which weighs eight pounds. As she's done filling the jug to make that long trek back home, a man who is a stranger stops her and asks for a drink of water. Does she get annoyed? Nope, she quickly offers him water.

Then she looks over to see he has 10 camels and offers to give each of them water. Camels can consume up to 30 gallons of water at a time. There were 10 camels and each one of them was thirsty, meaning they each would need at least 30 gallons of water...30×10...that was 300 hundred gallons of water! Can you imagine how tired she must have been just from thinking about all of the trips she would have to make to that well to quench the thirst of those camels? That didn't stop her from helping this man. She didn't stop until each of those camels' thirst was quenched.

This is a wonderful example of giving our best! As Christians, God expects us to give our all in whatever we do. Whether we are walking in love towards others or spending alone time with God, we are called to give our very best and go above and beyond. We should most definitely follow Rebekah's lead and do everything in excellence.

Prayer

Heavenly Father, forgive me for not putting forth my best in everything I do. From this point on help me to do everything in excellence whether or not I feel like it. Show me the areas in my life that are mediocre and need improvement.

What's the Tea?

Saffron Tea

According to the Centers for Disease Control and Prevention, approximately 735,000 Americans have a heart attack every year. What's even more heartbreaking is that 1 in 4 deaths in the United States are due to heart disease. These statistics show how critical it is for us to take care of our bodies and ensure that we have a healthy heart. In addition to eating healthy, exercising, and reducing stress, Saffron tea can further protect you against heart disease. The antioxidants and flavonoids in Saffron tea provide additional protection against heart disease.

Flavor Profile:

Saffron tea is brewed from the flowers of the saffron (*Crocus sativus*) plant, which is native to the Middle East and certain parts of Europe. Saffron tea has a strong, bitter flavor. It is recommended that this tea be mixed with another tea in order to cut the bitter taste.

Other Health Benefits:

Saffron tea not only helps protect the heart from disease, it also protects the eyes from damage caused by bright lights and deters the onset of blindness. Saffron tea is rich in properties that reduce the risk of cancer.

Other Teas to Try:

Other teas that reduce the risk of heart disease include:

- ❖ Cinnamon tea

- ❖ Turmeric tea

- ❖ Green tea

- ❖ Black tea

Day 20

RIGHTEOUSNESS

1 John 5:18 (NKJV)

This morning while driving to work, I was listening to a Dr. Tony Evans on the radio. He said something that really made me stop and think. He said, "Unrighteousness gives the enemy legal rights to you." I have always known that sin opened a door for the enemy to come into our lives and wreak all kinds of havoc. However, I've never thought of it in terms of legal rights to us.

According to the *Merriam Webster Dictionary*, a legal right is *"a claim recognized and delimited by law for the purpose of securing it."* Based on this definition, when we allow sin into our lives and move away from a life of righteousness to one of unrighteousness, the enemy is able to make a claim to our lives and take ownership of us. It is such a terrifying thought that a life of sin not only places us outside of God's will, but also out of His hands and protection, and into the hands of the enemy.

The only way to remain out of the enemy's grasp is by leading a life of righteousness. When we choose to walk in the spirit instead of the flesh, we choose to do what is pleasing to God instead of indulging our flesh. When we choose righteousness and holiness over sin, we demonstrate that we are children of God and we are secure in the hands of Christ. When we are in Christ, we belong to Him and the enemy can't have legal rights to us. This life on earth is far from easy. Every day is a battle to live a life of righteousness. There are so many distractions and temptations, but if we remain close to our Savior, we can overcome them all. As long as we seek Jesus and live holy as he did, we will remain in His protective embrace and the enemy can't claim us for himself. The enemy will be able to attack us, but he won't own us. We belong to Jesus as long as we commit to Him and walk in obedience.

Prayer

Jesus, make me holy and pure like You. Teach me how to live a life of righteousness. Help me to remain close to You, never turning my back on You to follow the ways of this world. I belong to You and want to remain Yours all the days of my life. Help me to not become distracted by the ways of this world. Help me to walk in obedience to You and live my life according to Your Word.

What's the Tea?

Nettle Tea

According to the American Society of Hematology, more than 3 million Americans are anemic. This blood disorder is the most common and is often seen in four different forms, which are iron deficiency anemia, aplastic anemia, hemolytic anemia, and sickle cell anemia. Of these four types of anemia, iron deficiency is the most common. In addition to increasing your iron intake in the form of pills to combat this form of anemia, you can also drink Nettle tea. Nettle tea contains iron, which makes it a great way to increase your iron intake and prevent iron deficiency anemia.

Flavor Profile:

Nettle tea is made from the leaves of the stinging nettle (*Urtica dioica*) plant. The stinging nettle plant is native to Europe, Asia, and North Africa. The flavor of Nettle tea can vary based on whether dried or fresh nettle leaves are used to make the tea. Nettle tea brewed from dried nettle leaves tends to be bitter, especially if steeped for a long time. When brewed from fresh herbs, Nettle tea tends to have a grassier flavor similar to spinach.

Other Health Benefits:

In addition to containing iron, Nettle tea is rich in calcium and magnesium. These high concentrations of minerals make Nettle tea helpful in preventing osteoporosis. Nettle tea also has analgesic and anti-inflammatory properties, making it a great way to relieve pain and inflammation. It also stimulates circulation in the body, which can also help relieve pain.

Other Teas to Try:

Other teas rich in iron and helpful in preventing iron deficiency anemia are:

- ❖ Red Raspberry Leaf tea
- ❖ Dandelion tea
- ❖ Yellow Dock tea
- ❖ Hawthorn tea

Day 21

PATIENCE IN AFFLICTION

Romans 12:12 (NIV)

We live in a society where we don't want to wait for anything. We want our food as fast as possible; we want our paychecks deposited into our accounts as soon as our employers release them, and we rather buy items on credit instead of waiting and saving up for it. At times, we let this mentality spill over into our lives as Christians.

Whenever problems arise in my life, I tend to become impatient. I want the issue to be resolved immediately or to get through the storm as quickly as possible. This, however, is not a realistic expectation. Most major issues or trials don't disappear quickly, but last for some time.

I believe that challenging situations last for a while because God uses them to teach us lessons and develop our character so that we become more like Him. One recurring lesson in my life has been patience. Today's scripture tells us that we are to be *"patient in affliction."* That is such a challenge for us as Christians because of the world we live in. We don't want to have to experience difficulties, and if we do, we want them to be over with immediately.

We have to move away from this worldly thinking of rushing through every problem, and learn to be patient. When we are patient during our affliction, a few things happen: we become more like Christ, our ability to be patient increases, we are able to endure our affliction with a joyful attitude, and we're able to persevere through our affliction stronger and better than before. The next time a problem arises in our lives, instead of trying to find the quickest way out of it, we should see it as an opportunity to grow in patience.

Prayer

Jesus, change my thinking from that of this world to Your thinking. Give me a mind like Yours so that when trials and tribulations arise, I greet them with patience instead of an attitude and a "get it over with" mentality. Help me to see the lessons You are trying to teach me in the midst of these storms instead of trying to find the quickest way out. Thank You for these opportunities of growth and character development.

What's the Tea?

Fennel Tea

Have you ever awakened in the morning with your eyes swollen and puffy? We usually wake up with our eyes puffy because we had a rough time sleeping the night before. Instead of going to work the next day looking like you had been crying all night, why not drink a cup of Fennel tea? Fennel tea has anti-inflammatory properties that allow it to rapidly reduce inflammation around the eyes. Fennel tea also has antibacterial properties and boosts your immune system. These properties help protect the eyes from infections, such as conjunctivitis.

Flavor Profile:

Fennel tea is brewed from the seeds of the fennel (*Foeniculum vulgare*) plant. The fennel plant is most often found in the Mediterranean. Fennel tea has a sweet flavor and slightly tastes like licorice. This tea is often confused with Anise tea.

Other Health Benefits:

Not only does Fennel tea help reduce puffiness around the eyes, it also helps relieve stomach spasms as well as other spasms throughout the body. Fennel tea contains antibacterial, antiseptic, and antifungal properties, making it an excellent immune booster. Fennel tea also helps fight bad breath.

Other Teas to Try:

Other teas that have anti-inflammatory properties are:

- ❖ Cinnamon tea

- ❖ Graviola tea

- ❖ Turmeric tea

- ❖ White Willow tea

Day 22

CONSISTENCY

Daniel 6:1-12 (NKJV)

When chaos overtakes your life, what happens to your relationship with Christ? Does Jesus become a distant thought while the problems at hand move to the forefront of your mind? Does your quiet time with the Lord become so infrequent that days pass by before you realize that you haven't spoken to Him or spent time in His Word?

There are times in our lives when certain trials shake us to our core. Maybe our financial situation is getting worse even though we've been tithing and keeping to our budget. Maybe a relationship we believed was headed towards marriage came to an unexpected end leaving us heartbroken. Situations like these sometimes shake our faith and cause us to question whether God is truly with us and for us. The enemy wants us to let these circumstances cause our faith to waver so that we will turn away from God.

During the low points in our lives, we should follow Daniel's example. Even though Daniel faced being thrown into the den of lions, he didn't get angry with God or pull back from Him. He remained faithful to God and consistent in his prayer life. When problems arise in our lives, we need to continue to seek God like we did before. We can't let frustration, disappointment, fear, or discouragement cause us to retreat from Him.

When we remain faithful to God during our trials and tribulations, He will be faithful to us and bring us through victorious. Just like God didn't allow the lions to eat Daniel (*Daniel 6:22, NKJV*), He won't allow challenging times to destroy us. We need to do our part by continuing to pursue Him daily and putting our trust in Him despite our circumstances. Consistency is key.

Prayer

Heavenly Father, strengthen my faith and trust in You so that my relationship with You doesn't falter just because trials and tribulations occur in my life. Help me to remain faithful to You despite my circumstances. Help me to know and believe that You are always with me.

What's the Tea?

Peppermint Tea

Spring is such a beautiful time of the year. The sun comes out and brings just the right amount of warmth, and flowers are in full bloom. Although it is such a magnificent sight, the pollen and other allergens spring brings are not too friendly to those who easily get sinus infections. Although there are many medications that are available to combat sinus issues, a natural remedy that is just as effective is Peppermint tea. Peppermint tea contains menthol, which naturally relieves congestion. The menthol in Peppermint tea relieves sinus pressure due to colds and allergies, and it helps soothe sore throats, which sometimes accompany sinus infections.

Flavor Profile:

Peppermint tea is made from the leaves of the peppermint (*Mentha piperita*) plant. This plant is a blend of water and spearmint. The peppermint plant originates from Europe, but is used widely across the globe. Peppermint tea has a refreshing mint flavor and is caffeine free.

Other Health Benefits:

In addition to fighting sinus infections, Peppermint tea has been known to reduce fevers because of the menthol it contains. The menthol in Peppermint tea helps to cool one's body down internally. Peppermint tea also fights bad breath, strengthens the immune system, and helps prevent vomiting, nausea, and motion sickness.

Other Teas to Try:

If you're not a fan of peppermint tea or are allergic, there are other teas that help relieve sinus infections. Some of these teas include:

- ❖ Ginger tea
- ❖ Thyme tea
- ❖ Sage tea
- ❖ Elderberry tea

Day 23

KNOWING
ABBA'S VOICE

John 10:27 (AMP)

Have you ever watched how a baby responds to their mother or father's voice? The baby's eyes become wide with excitement, a large grin spreads across their face, they begin to coo, and they turn their head in the direction of their parent's voice in hopes that they will see them. Babies respond this way because they know their parents' voice.

Just like an infant knows their parents' voice, we are to know our Abba's voice. How can we hear from our Heavenly Father if we don't know His voice? How can we be led by Him if we don't know His voice? We can't truly know God if we don't know His voice. We don't know God's voice by simply claiming to be a Christian or by only attending church. Just like a newborn child has to learn their parents' voice, we have to learn our

Heavenly Father's voice.

One way we can know God's voice is by belonging to Him (*John 8:47, NLT*). We belong to God after we have accepted Christ as our Lord and Savior, and we walk in obedience by obeying His Word. The only way we can obey God is by spending time in His Word. When we spend time in His Word, not only do we learn how to obey God, but we also learn His voice through His scriptures. God's Word is His words to us. It only makes sense that if we spend time reading His Word that we are able to hear and know His voice.

In order to know God's voice, we must come to Him with our ears open and ready to listen (*Isaiah 55:3, NLT*). If we come to God with the mindset that we're going to pick and choose what we're going to listen to, then we will never truly know His voice. We must come to Him willing to listen to everything He has to say, even if we may not like what He has to say. We can't come to Him with an attitude or stubbornness, but we must be ready to submit to His will.

We need to learn God's voice so that we can hear from Him. If we don't know His voice, we will be misled and will be outside of God's will for our lives. The only way we can truly know His voice is by spending time with Him and by putting aside our pride and "know-it-all" attitude. When we come humbly before Him ready to listen, then we will truly know His voice.

Prayer

Heavenly Father, teach me to know how to hear from You. Make Your voice clear and distinctive to me. I always want to know when You're speaking to me. Open my ears so that I can hear You always.

What's the Tea?

Ginkgo Biloba Tea

Have you ever walked into a room to do something and when you got there, you completely forgot what you intended to do? Or maybe a friend or your spouse asked you to do something and 15 minutes later you can't remember what their request was? I don't know about you, but I hate when my memory fails me. I feel so frustrated when I can't remember something. One way to help improve your memory is by drinking Ginkgo Biloba tea. Ginkgo Biloba tea has been found to improve both memory and concentration. Ginkgo Biloba helps increase antioxidant activity, decreases oxidative pressure, and improves overall brain circulation all of which are critical to overall cognitive health.

Flavor Profile:

Ginkgo Biloba tea is brewed from the dried leaves of the Gingko or Maidenhair tree. This plant is native to Eastern China. Ginkgo Biloba tea has a dull flavor, which is why it is often paired with other herbs such as cinnamon or lemon peel.

Other Health Benefits:

Ginkgo Biloba tea is also known for reducing risk for dementia and Alzheimer's disease. This tea helps reduce anxiety and depression, reverse the effects of allergic reactions, and helps relieve pain caused by migraines.

Other Teas to Try:

Other teas that aid in improving memory are:

- ❖ Green tea

- ❖ Sage tea

- ❖ Rosemary tea

- ❖ Gotu Kola tea

Day 24

WHAT ARE
YOUR EYES SEEING?

Philippians 4:8 (NKJV)

Have you ever watched a commercial and when the commercial was over you wanted what was being advertised? Or maybe you saw someone eating a delicious meal and you start craving that exact meal? In these instances, what we see influences our desires so easily.

What we watch greatly influences how we think and behave. According to Matthew 6:22-23 *"The eye is a lamp of the body. So, if your eye is healthy, your whole body will be full of light, but if your eye is bad, your whole body will be full of darkness. If then the light in you is darkness, how great is the darkness!"* This verse is telling us that what we watch or see influences us. Our behaviors, our thoughts, our words, everything is affected by what we allow into our body via what we watch or see. What we expose our eyes to can influence our thinking and actions for good or for worse. We truly have to be mindful of what movies and TV shows we are watching, what books we are reading, and who we're hanging out with. Each of these and so much more can influence the way we live our lives.

So, what should we expose our eyes to that will influence us for the best? According to *Philippians 4:8 (NKJV)*, we should be thinking on anything that is true, pure, and loving. Basically, anything that lines up with God's Word and doesn't contradict His Word in any way, shape, or form is what we should be exposing ourselves to. Before deciding to watch a movie or show, read a book, or go to certain places, we need to view it behind the lens of God's Word. If it contradicts God's Word and is leading us to sin against God, we need to leave it alone.

In order for us to be filled with the light of Christ, we have to be mindful of what we our exposing our eyes to. If we are constantly exposing ourselves to the things of this world, our flesh will rule us and we will be filled with darkness. Let's make sure that we are examining all things against God's Word so that we can be filled with His light and be the light in this dark world.

Prayer

Jesus, help me to be more mindful of what I am exposing my eyes to. I want to be filled with Your light Lord, so keep me aware of what I watch and see. If it contradicts You and Your Word, give me the strength to leave it alone so that I will not become filled with darkness. I don't want to be like this world. I want to be like You in all that I say and do.

What's the Tea?

Tulsi Tea

Have you ever been at work and noticed that your breath is a little tart? You brushed your teeth that morning, but maybe your lunch took away that minty fresh breath. Often, to rectify this issue, we're quick to grab a piece of gum and pop it in our mouth. I don't know about you, but I feel that most gum doesn't provide a long-lasting effect or simply does not cut it. One way to stop bad breath is drinking a cup of Tulsi tea. Tulsi tea contains antimicrobial properties, which combat germs and bacteria found in the oral cavity. By stopping germs and bacteria found in the mouth, Tulsi tea both prevents bad breath and serves as a mouthwash. Tulsi tea also aids in preventing other dental and oral conditions including pyorrhea, mouth ulcers, and oral cancer.

Flavor Profile:

Tulsi (*Ocimum tenuiflorum or Ocimum sanctum*) is native to India. It is often referred to as holy basil. The Tulsi plant grows as a branched shrub that grows up to 60cm tall with furry stems, aromatic purple or green leaves, and small white or purplish flowers that grow on the edge of the branches. The leaves are dried in order to make Tulsi tea. Tulsi tea has a strong scent and an astringent flavor. It is sometimes bitter and can have a floral and peppery taste. Certain varieties of Tulsi tea have a clove-like aromatic scent and spiced flavor.

Other Health Benefits:

In addition to curing halitosis and other dental and oral health conditions, Tulsi tea aids in treating coughs, bronchitis, asthma, and other respiratory conditions. This is due to the various properties Tulsi tea has. Tulsi tea has immuno-modulatory properties, which helps boost the immune system; antitussive properties, which helps suppress coughs; and expectorant properties, which helps remove phlegm. Other health benefits include relieving fevers and reducing stress.

Other Teas to Try:

Other teas that help fight bad breath and aid in dental health are:

- ❖ Peppermint tea
- ❖ Cinnamon tea

- ❖ Ginger tea

- ❖ Green tea

Day 25

JEALOUSY

John 3:23-30

Jealousy, a trap that's fairly easy to fall into without even realizing it. When we focus on how God is using our brothers and sisters in Christ to glorify His name and build the Kingdom of Heaven, we can succumb to jealousy if we compare our lives to theirs. Instead of celebrating our siblings in Christ, we may begin to feel slighted and useless. Out of a jealousy-filled heart, we may even begin to criticize and ridicule them.

Today's reading shows us how even as Christians we can be overtaken by jealousy. John the Baptist's disciples were upset because many of the Jews were going to Jesus to be baptized instead of coming to them. These disciples got caught up in the flesh and let jealousy prevent them from celebrating the amazing work Jesus was doing. Instead of praising God for all of the people that were coming to know Christ as their Savior and getting baptized, the felt slighted and unimportant because they weren't the ones sharing the Gospel and baptizing these unbelievers.

John the Baptist's disciples allowed jealousy into their hearts because they took their eyes off of God and began to focus on themselves. Reaching and baptizing the lost was no longer about adding to the Kingdom of Heaven. In their hearts, they made it about themselves and about what they were doing. When we focus on ourselves instead of on God, we begin to think that our contributions to God's Kingdom are our own doing. Any and everything we do is because God has equipped us to do it; it is not because of our own might, strength, or wisdom.

John the Baptist's response to his disciples shows us what our attitude should be towards our brothers and sisters in Christ who are being used greatly by God. We need to be humble like John and know that first and foremost that this life is about Jesus and building His Kingdom. It's not about us. We need to celebrate with our siblings in Christ when they accomplish anything for God's glory.

If we keep our eyes off of ourselves and focus on doing what God has called us to do, we will be joyful when our siblings in Christ succeed. We need to remember that

God is working through each of us to reach the lost. When we become jealous of our brothers and sisters in Christ, we are actually jealous of the God in them. So let's take our eyes off of what everyone else is doing, put our eyes on God, and do what He has called us to do.

Prayer

Jesus, remove any remnants of jealousy in my heart. Forgive me for being jealous of any of my brothers and sisters in Christ. Fix my eyes on You instead of what everyone else is doing. Help me to focus on what You have called me to do and to do it for Your glory. Help me to know and believe that my role in building the Kingdom of Heaven is just as important as every other role.

What's the Tea?

Turmeric Tea

In the U.S., approximately 31.6 million people have been diagnosed with some form of eczema. Although there are many products available to treat eczema, one natural remedy is Turmeric tea. Turmeric tea treats various skin conditions including eczema. This tea also helps reduce the inflammation that is often associated with eczema.

Flavor Profile:

Turmeric (*Curcuma longa*) is native to India and Southeast Asian countries. The dried root of the Turmeric plant is ground into a powder and then added to boiling water to create Turmeric tea. Fresh turmeric can also be sliced and boiled in hot water to make fresh Turmeric tea. Since Turmeric tea has such a bitter taste, it is recommended that it be sweetened with honey or served as a base for another tea, such as Black tea, to help dilute the flavor.

Other Health Benefits:

Turmeric tea also provides other health benefits including relieving arthritis, swelling and inflammation, preventing Alzheimer's disease, and preventing cancer. This tea also serves as an immune system booster and helps lower cholesterol.

Other Teas to Try:

Other teas that treat skin disorders such as eczema include:

- ❖ Burdock tea
- ❖ Fumitory tea
- ❖ Red Clover tea
- ❖ Lavender tea

Day 26

THINKING WE KNOW
MORE THAN GOD

Isaiah 55:8-9 (MSG)

Have you ever reached a point in your life where you felt stuck? It seemed like no matter what you did you couldn't make a move. You tried to go left, right, forwards, backwards, up, down, and around, and no matter what direction you went in you ran smack dab into a wall. What do we do when we feel stuck? How do we respond? Is there something that we are doing that is preventing God from moving us forward in our lives? I have felt stuck during various seasons of my life. It seemed like any move I would make, any plan I would make...literally anything I did would not succeed.

During my season of being "stuck," I started being hard on myself because I felt like a failure since I wasn't at a certain point in my life. I had wanted so much more out of life, but I felt as if no matter what I would do to try to move forward, I could not budge. God eventually revealed to me why I was stuck: *I kept trying to make my plans God's plans. I kept trying to push my agenda on God. I thought that I knew better than Him.* Although I never mentally or verbally expressed this, my heart and actions showed that I believed that I knew what was best for me and that I could come up with a better plan for my life than God.

God doesn't need us to map out our lives or try to figure everything out. He already has incredible plans for us. *Jeremiah 1:5 (MSG)* tells us "*Before I shaped you in the womb, I knew all about you. Before you saw the light of day, I had holy plans for you: a prophet to the nations – that's what I had in mind for you.*" This scripture is telling us that even before we were conceived, God knew His plans for our lives. He knew what He called us to do. He knew how each and every day of our lives would turn out. He knew everything about us before we were even thought of by our parents.

When we are feeling stuck or are unhappy with where we are in life, we should not be discouraged. God has great plans for us. He will fulfill the plans and purposes He has for our lives. Our main responsibility is to continue to pursue God, walk in complete obedience to Him, trust His timing, and wait on Him with an abundance of patience and joy.

Prayer

Lord, I am so grateful that You have always known me. You have known me even before I was conceived. I thank You for making an incredible plan for my life, a plan that I can't even begin to fathom. Lord, even though my life isn't where I want it to be right now, I thank You that You know what is best and that the best is yet to come.

What's the Tea?

Matcha Tea

No one ever wants to be told by their doctor that they have high cholesterol. High cholesterol can harm your arteries, lead to heart disease, and put you more at risk for having a stroke. One tea that helps improve cholesterol is Matcha tea. When consumed regularly, Matcha tea helps lower levels of LDL (harmful) cholesterol and increases levels of HDL (good) cholesterol.

Flavor Profile:

Matcha originated in China in the 9th century. Matcha is made from the tencha leaf, which is shade grown and high quality. The leaves of the tencha plant are kept hidden to keep from being exposed to direct sunlight, which slows the process of photosynthesis and stunts the growth of the plants. This process causes the leaves to have a dark shade of green and stimulates the formation of chlorophyll and amino acids. The youngest and smallest leaves are used to produce the highest quality tea. The leaves are then steamed, which prevents oxidation and preserves the flavor and nutritional value. Once this step is completed, the leaves are ground into an ultra-fine powder, which is used to brew Matcha tea. Matcha tea has a unique flavor due to the chlorophyll and amino acids it contains. It has a slight vegetative taste followed by an astringent flavor with a hint of sweetness lingering at the end. Because of its unique flavor, Matcha tea often does not require milk or honey and lemon to sweeten its taste.

Other Health Benefits:

Just like many other teas, Matcha tea contains antioxidants and polyphenols, which help boost the immune system. Matcha tea also helps manage type-2 diabetes, serves as an energy booster, helps one to relax, increases mental alertness, and protects from certain infections.

Other Teas to Try:

Other teas that help lower bad cholesterol and increase good cholesterol include:

- ❖ Hibiscus tea

- ❖ Rooibos tea

- ❖ Redbush tea

- ❖ Ginger tea

- ❖ Vanilla tea

- ❖ Ginseng tea

Day 27

FUMBLING
THROUGH THE DARK

John 8:12

Have you ever tried to search for something in the dark? I've done this on many occasions. Usually if I'm rushing in the morning and I leave my phone in the room, I quickly run to my room and instead of turning on the lights, I fumble around with my hands in hopes that I will quickly grab it. At times I find my phone with no problem. More often than not I usually trip over a bag or a pair of shoes, hit my shin on the corner of my bed frame, or bump my knee on my dresser. It's hard to navigate an area if you can't see where you're going. Just like it's difficult and sometimes painful to search for items in the dark, it's also a challenge to navigate this dark world we live in without the Light of the World.

In today's verse, we read that Jesus is the light of the world. The world we live in is very dark spiritually. This world has strived so hard to remove God, His Word, and His Son Jesus from it, and because of that, this world is filled with darkness. Just turn on the news and we can see so much evil in this world. At times it's very discouraging, depressing, and overwhelming. This is why we need Jesus. His light brightens this dark world. His light makes it so that we can see in the midst of all the darkness. We don't have to navigate through the darkness of this world. Jesus will not only brighten this world, but He will light our path so that we can see where we are going. Being in His light fills us with hope and joy. His light allows us to see the traps of the enemy so that we do not fall prey to them. His light uplifts and encourages us, especially when we feel like giving up.

Since the world we live in is filled with darkness, it will try to destroy our joy and peace, it will try to discourage us and get us to quit. However, if we follow Jesus, His light will brighten our lives and will encourage us to press forward despite the state of this world. When His light shines brightly in us, we can be a light to this dark world that desperately needs Jesus (*Matthew 5:16, NKJV*).

Prayer

Jesus, let Your light shine brightly in my life so that I won't be consumed by this dark world. Keep me from succumbing to discouragement when I see the evil in this world. Instead, help me to let Your light in me shine radiantly so that this dark world can be exposed to You and Your glorious light. I pray that Your light strengthens my hope in You and encourages this dark world to put their hope and faith in You.

What's the Tea?

Vanilla Tea

I don't know about you, but I get carsick fairly easily. I can be sitting in the car and all of a sudden, a strong feeling of nausea overwhelms me. Sometimes it is so bad that taking deep breaths or opening the car window to get fresh air does nothing to help relieve the nausea. One way to help naturally curb the urge to hurl is by drinking a cup of Vanilla tea. Vanilla tea has been found to relieve feelings of nausea, prevent vomiting, and calm an upset stomach.

Flavor Profile:

Vanilla tea is brewed from the beans of the vanilla (*Vanilla planifolia*) plant. The vanilla plant is native to Central America and Mexico. Vanilla tea has a strong, sweet scent that is often mistaken for fresh-baked cookies.

Other Health Benefits:

In addition to relieving nausea, Vanilla tea reduces

cholesterol levels, strengthens hair and encourages hair growth, and prevents acne due to its antibacterial properties. The scent of vanilla promotes feelings of calmness and reduces anxiety.

Other Teas to Try:

Other teas known to prevent vomiting include:

- ❖ Ginger tea

- ❖ German Chamomile tea

- ❖ Peppermint tea

- ❖ Red Raspberry Leaf tea

Day 28

GOD, MY HELPER

Hebrews 13:6

Are you the type of person that always expects the worse? Maybe you tend to think of the worst possible scenario so that you can mentally prepare for any problems that may arise? Maybe you attribute this behavior to being a realist. How do you feel when you imagine these scenarios in which everything goes horribly wrong? Do you feel joy and peace? Or do you become overwhelmed by feelings of anxiety and discouragement?

At times, I catch myself thinking of the worst that could possibly happen in a situation. When I'm done playing the scenario over in my head, I often feel drained and I begin to worry. In *1 Peter 5:7*, we are told to cast *"all your anxieties on Him, because He cares for you."* Giving your anxieties to the Lord means to submit your worries and fears to God. It's not our responsibility to brace ourselves for the worst that could happen. We are to give it to God and to trust Him to work it all out in our favor. Worrying only steals our joy and peace. Worry makes the situation worse instead of improving it.

Today's verse tells us that the Lord is our Helper. Since the all-mighty, all-knowing, powerful God is our Helper, why would we let worry and fear control us? Since God is ultimately in control, we must rest in Him and trust Him to bring us through any and all situations that occur in our lives. We must stop worrying and letting fear dictate our lives. That's not living as a child of God. Our Heavenly Father knows our future and because we are His children by faith in Jesus Christ, He will bring us through triumphantly.

Prayer

Lord, help me to remember to call on You instead of worrying. Strengthen my faith and trust in You. You know how best to handle any situations that occur in my life. Help me to lean on You instead of on worry or fear in my time of trouble. You guide my footsteps, and You know my beginning to my end. I will trust You, Lord.

What's the Tea?

Mullein Tea

Approximately 26 million Americans are diagnosed with asthma. Of the 26 million Americans, 18.9 million are adults and 7.1 million are children. Individuals who suffer from asthma experience chronic inflammation that occurs in the lungs and leads to coughing, tightness in the chest, wheezing and shortness of breath. With each passing year, the number of Americans diagnosed with asthma increases. A natural way to fight asthma is by drinking Mullein tea. Mullein tea promotes the elimination of mucus and other fluid from the respiratory tract. It also possesses healing properties, which soothe the mucus membranes. These properties make Mullein tea excellent for fighting lung conditions such as asthma.

Flavor Profile:

Mullein tea is an herbal tea that is made by brewing the leaves and flowers of the Mullein (*Verbascum thapsus*) plant. The Mullein plant, which is often mistaken for a weed, is a flowering plant native to Europe, Asia, and

142

North Africa. Mullein tea has a faint sweet flavor with a hint of spice.

Other Health Benefits:

Not only does Mullein tea aid in treating asthma, it treats certain skin conditions and joint pain, heals eye infections, balances hormones, and soothes throbbing headaches. Mullein tea is able to treat certain skin conditions and joint pain with its antioxidants that strengthen the immune system and prevent chronic inflammation, which causes skin conditions and joint pain. Mullein tea balances hormones by treating many of the side effects of an underactive thyroid gland.

Other Teas to Try:

Other teas that treat lung conditions include:

- ❖ Calendula tea
- ❖ Fennel tea
- ❖ Licorice tea
- ❖ Pineapple tea

Day 29

A ROOT OF BITTERNESS

Hebrews 12:15 (NLT)

Have you ever met someone that always seems to have a nasty attitude? Maybe they respond to everything negatively or with anger. Have you ever wondered what led to that person becoming that way, filled with so much anger and bitterness?

Today's verse tells us to make sure that we do not allow a *"poisonous root of bitterness"* to come into our lives. The fact that the Bible describes bitterness as poisonous shows us that bitterness is not good for us. If we were to be bitten by a poisonous snake or insect, that poison would get into our bloodstream and spread throughout our entire body. Our organs would be affected and eventually our bodies would shut down if we weren't given an antidote. Bitterness has that same effect on our lives. It impacts every aspect of our lives from our way of thinking to how we interact with others.

According to the Oxford Dictionary, bitterness means "anger and disappointment at being treated unfairly; resentment." Bitterness is rooted in anger and hurt. This means that when someone wrongs us and we choose not to forgive them, we allow bitterness to begin to take root in our hearts. The more we walk in unforgiveness, the more our hearts become hardened and filled with bitterness.

When our hearts are filled with bitterness, it affects every aspect of our lives. It makes us mean, causes us to have a bad attitude, prevents us from showing mercy, and keeps us from walking in love. In addition to that, it makes it hard to maintain friendships and relationships since we are unable to forgive those who hurt us.

So how can we guard ourselves from a root of bitterness? *Ephesians 4:31-32* tells us, *"Let all bitterness and wrath and anger and clamor and slander be put away from you, along with all malice. Be kind to one another, tenderhearted, forgiving one another, as God in Christ forgave you."* This verse is telling us to let go of any bitterness or anger and instead to walk in love towards everyone and to forgive just as God has forgiven us. Any time someone mistreats us, we need to address the issue with him or her immediately in a loving manner and forgive them. We are not to hold on to our anger towards them. We need to let it go and move forward.

Prayer

Jesus, help me to choose to forgive instead of choosing to hold a grudge against those who wrong me. Even though what they did left me hurt and bruised, help me to see them through Your loving eyes and to extend mercy and kindness towards them instead of anger and hostility. Guard my heart against a poisonous root of bitterness and hardness.

What's the Tea?

Pineapple Tea

Have you ever had one of those days where you feel like your mood is just dragging? No matter what someone says or does, you can't seem to shake the cloud of gloom surrounding you. If you have ever had an experience like this, Pineapple tea may be just what you need. Pineapple tea has been known to help boost one's mood. Pineapple tea is high in Vitamin C. Research has shown that when individuals with Vitamin C deficiency increase their Vitamin C intake, their mood improves. Maybe you're like me and don't always like the awful taste of most Vitamin C tablets. Try incorporating a cup of Pineapple tea to reap the same benefits.

Flavor Profile:

Pineapples are native to Brazil and Paraguay. Pineapple tea can be made by boiling the pineapple peel or fresh pineapple. Pineapple tea has a citrus aroma and a sweet yet tart flavor. This tea is often paired with other teas, such as Green tea, Lemongrass tea, Ginger tea, and

Chamomile tea.

Other Health Benefits:

In addition to enhancing one's mood, Pineapple tea has can also help reduce inflammation. Pineapples contain bromelain, which is an enzyme that decreases inflammation. Other health benefits include promoting weight loss with its metabolism boosting effects and strengthening the immune system.

Other Teas to Try:

Other teas that possess mood enhancing properties are:

- ❖ Sage tea
- ❖ Turmeric tea
- ❖ Green tea
- ❖ Dandelion tea

Day 30

RESPONDING TO
GOD'S PROMISES

2 Peter 1:5-7 (NKJV)

This morning while reading *2 Peter 1*, God began to minister to me about His promises to us and when we don't experience those promises in our lives. Today's verse tells us that we have to *respond* to God's promises in order to access them. It even tells us exactly how we need to respond so that we can tap into God's promises to us.

I used to think that all I had to do was have enough faith for God's promises to become real in my life, but today's verse tells us otherwise. In addition to faith, we have seven other responsibilities we must commit to in order to tap into the incredible promises of God. These include *"virtue, knowledge, self-control, perseverance, godliness, brotherly kindness, and love."*

Virtue refers to how we live our lives. In order for God's promises to be real in our lives, we must live a life of moral excellence, and walk in obedience to God and His word. We are called to a higher standard and our lives must demonstrate this. Knowledge indicates how well we know God and the things of Him. We must seek to know God intimately and personally; we must seek to know His will for our lives. Self-control refers to how we keep our flesh under submission to our spirit and mind. Our flesh wants to do what's wrong and longs for the things of this world. We cannot let our flesh rule us or it will lead to death spiritually and physically (*Romans 8:13, AMP*).

Perseverance indicates our willingness to continue on the right path despite what problems come our way. The Greek word for perseverance is proskartereō, which means *"to be steadfast, to continue steadfastly in a thing and give unremitting care to it."* God calls us to persevere in our relationship with Him, our faith, and our commitment to Him to this extent. We can't halfway do it and expect Him to fulfill His promises in our lives. Godliness refers to living a holy, pure life just as God is holy and pure *(1 Peter 1:15-16, NKJV)*.

Although brotherly kindness and love sound like they are one in the same, they refer to two different things. Brotherly kindness refers to our relationship with other believers. We are to walk in love towards our brothers and sisters in Christ, and are to love them like we would love a biological sibling. Love refers to walking in love towards non-believers. It's easy to love those who are kind to us, but what about those who mistreat us and seem to go out of their way to make our lives miserable? We are called to love those who mistreat us even when we feel like they don't deserve it. Once we start fulfilling these seven other responsibilities, then we can truly begin to experience the promises of God in our lives.

Prayer

Jesus, thank You for showing me that it's not enough to have faith, but that You require more of me. I thank You Lord that You will help me to live a virtuous and holy life, that You will help me to exercise self-control in every area of my life, that You will help me to continue to press forward in my relationship with You and not give up just because things are getting tough, that You will help me to walk in love towards both my siblings in Christ and those who have yet to become a part of Your family. I thank You Lord that as I do my part, you will do Your part and will fulfill Your promises to me.

What's the Tea?

Chamomile Tea

According to the American Diabetes Association, approximately 1.25 million Americans have been diagnosed with type 1 diabetes. This statistic includes both children and adults. In 2015, 30.3 million Americans reported being diagnosed with diabetes. Every year 1.5 million Americans are diagnosed with diabetes. Diabetes impacts your body's ability to make or use insulin and can cause your body to experience various symptoms. Some of these symptoms can include increased risk of stroke, loss of consciousness, visual impairment, risk of infections, and high blood pressure. With the risk of these side effects, it is imperative that those with diabetes manage their blood sugar levels. Research studies have shown that Chamomile tea is effective in reducing blood sugar levels and balancing the amount of insulin in the body. The nutrients in Chamomile tea help prevent extreme lows and highs in blood sugar levels.

Flavor Profile:

The name chamomile originated from the Greek term *chamai melon*, which means ground apple. Chamomile tea is made by brewing the flowers of the Chamomile (*Anthemis nobilis or Matricaria recutita*) plant. Chamomile tea has a scent similar to crisp apples. It has a sweet flavor of apples with a light, flowery taste.

Other Health Benefits:

Chamomile tea is widely known for its relaxation effects. It is often recommended to drink as a sleep aid, and it helps reduce stress and anxiety, which promotes relaxation. Chamomile tea also has anti-inflammatory properties, which aids in improving digestion.

Other Teas to Try:

Other teas known to help lower blood sugar levels are

- ❖ Green tea

- ❖ Black tea

- ❖ Oolong tea

- ❖ Bilberry tea

REFERENCES

"About Matcha." Matcha Source.
< https://matchasource.com/about-matcha/ >

"Anemia." American Society of Hematology.
<https://www.hematology.org/Patients/Anemia/>

"Asthma Facts." American College of Allergy, Asthma, Immunology.
< https://acaai.org/news/facts-statistics/asthma >

Axe, Josh. "Ginkgo Biloba Benefits Energy, Mood, & Memory." Dr. Axe Food is Medicine.
https://draxe.com/ginkgo-biloba-benefits/#>

Axe, Josh. "Turmeric Curcumin: Can This Herb Really Combat Disease?" Dr. Axe Food is Medicine.
< https://draxe.com/turmeric-curcumin-benefits/#>

Axe, Josh. "9 Echinacea Benefits from Colds to Cancer." Dr. Axe Food is Medicine.
< https://draxe.com/echinacea-benefits/#>

"Bitterness." English Oxford Living Dictionaries. "
https://www.lexico.com/en/definition/bitterness >

Boling, Janice. "Tips for Treating Earaches and Ear

Infections with Medicinal Herbs." Every Green Herb.
<https://www.everygreenherb.com/earache.html>

Branch, Solomon. "The Best Herbal Tea for Nausea." Livestrong.< https://www.livestrong.com/article/479396-the-best-herbal-tea-for-nausea/>

Bryan, Derek. "Health Benefits of Honeybush Tea." Livestrong. <https://www.livestrong.com/article/257007-health-benefits-of-honeybush-tea/>

Cathy. "Mulberry Leaf Tea Part 1-Fresh." Wordpress. <https://cohlinn.wordpress.com/2013/05/05/mulberry-leaf-tea/>

Chandler, Brynne. "Rosehip & Hibiscus Tea Benefits." SFGate. <https://healthyeating.sfgate.com/rosehip-hibiscus-tea-benefits-7016.html>

Cherney, Kristeen; Pietrangelo, Ann. "The Effects of Diabetes on Your Body." Healthline. <https://www.health-line.com/health/diabetes/effects-on-body#1>

Chew, Norma. "What Are the Health Benefits of Sage Tea?"Livestrong. < https://www.livestrong.com/article/96369-health-benefits-sage-tea/>

Chittenden, Brent. "Mulberry Tea: Nutrition, Benefits, & Side Effects Explained." Foods For Better Health. <https://www.foodsforbetterhealth.com/mulberry-tea-nutrition-facts-benefits-side-effects-30313>

Contursi, Janet. "Herbal Tea & Eczema." healthfully. < https://healthfully.com/440991-herbal-tea-eczema.html >

"Delight in Cinnamon." The Republic of Tea Leading Purveyor of Premium Teas.

< http://the.republicoftea.com/teablog/delight-in-cinnamon/>

Dolan, Carly. "22 Health Benefits of Ginger Root & Ginger Tea." HealthWholeness.com.
< https://healthwholeness.com/ginger-benefits/>

Douglas, Ellen. "The Benefits of Horsetail Tea." Livestrong.
< https://www.livestrong.com/article/128729-benefits-horsetail-tea/>

"Echinacea Tea and Its Benefits." Drink Herbal Tea.com.
<www.drinkherbaltea.com/echinacea-tea/>

"Echinacea Tea-Get an Immune System Boost." The Right Tea.
< https://www.therighttea.com/echinacea-tea.html>

"Eczema Facts." National Eczema Association.
< https://nationaleczema.org/research/eczema-facts/>

Editorial Team. "Matcha GreenTea: 10 Amazing Benefits of This Japanese Elixir." Natural Living Ideas.
< https://www.naturallivingideas.com/matcha-green-tea/>

Foster, Kelli. "Inside the Spice Cabinet: Fennel Seed." Kitchn.< https://www.thekitchn.com/inside-the-spice-cabinet-fennel-seed-109077>

Frey, Malia. "Honeybush Tea Benefits and Side Effects." Verywell-fit.
< https://www.verywellfit.com/honeybush-tea-benefits-and-side-effects-4163882>

G., Alexa. "15 Insane Health Benefits of Tulsi Tea: Distress with this super herb." Tea Mind Body.
<https://www.teamindbody.com/blogs/healthy-tea-

info/9885490-15-insane-health-benefits-of-tulsi-tea-de-stress-with-this-super-herb>

"Ginkgo Biloba Tea Benefits." TeaBenefits.com.
< http://www.teabenefits.com/ginkgo-biloba-tea-benefits.html >

Godinez, Brenda. "10 Powerful Benefits Of Drinking Moringa Every Day." mgbfood.
<https://www.mindbodygreen.com/0-22401/10-powerful-benefits-of-drinking-moringa-every-day.html>

Goldman, Rena. "Saffron Tea: 5 Benefits and How to Make it."healthline.
< https://www.healthline.com/health/food-nutrition/saffron-tea-benefits#1>

Gotter, Ana. "7 Ways Turmeric Tea Benefits Your Health." Healthline.
< https://www.healthline.com/health/turmeric-tea-benefits#boosts-the-immune-system6>

Hayim, Lisa. "Benefits of Hibiscus Tea." mbgfood.
< https://www.mindbodygreen.com/articles/benefits-of-hibiscus-tea >

"Heart Disease Facts." Centers for Disease Control and Prevention.
< https://www.cdc.gov/heartdisease/facts.htm >

"Herbal Tea."TeaSpring.com.
< http://www.teaspring.com/Chrysanthemum.asp >

"Herbal Tea." TeaSpring.com.
<http://www.teaspring.com/Lavendar.asp >

"High Blood Pressure Facts." Centers for Disease Control and

Prevention.< https://www.cdc.gov/bloodpressure/facts.htm>

"How Many Gallons of Water Can a Camel Drink?" Reference.< https://www.reference.com/pets-animals/many-gallons-water-can-camel-drink-2c89d517ec357f47>

"Improve Your Health with Horsetail Tea." Horsetail Tea. <www.horse-tailtea.net>

Jewell, Tim; McDermott, Annette. "Can Herbal Teas Lower My Cholesterol?" Healthline.
< https://www.healthline.com/health/high-cholesterol/herbal-tea#tea-and-cholesterol3>

Jewitt, Angela. *Types of Tea and Their Health Benefits*, Whytbank Publishing. Johnson, Aimable. "9 Proven Health Benefits of Rooibos Tea." VegKitchen.
<https://www.vegkitchen.com/9-proven-health-benefits-of-rooibos-tea/>

K., Nina. "Benefits of Drinking Ginger Tea." Livestrong.
< https://livestrong.com/article/272999-benefits-of-drinking-ginger-tea/>

Kelsey, Amber. "Chrysanthemum Tea Benefits." Livestrong.
<https://livestrong.com/article/461896-chrysanthemum-tea-benefits/>

Keplinger, Carrie. "Boost Your Immune System with Teas High in Vitamin C."
< https://thedailytea.com/wellness/boost-immune-teas-high-in-vitamin-c/

Khemka, Tulsi. "How would you describe the taste of cinnamon?" Quora. < https://www.quora.com/How-would-you-describe-the-taste-of-cinnamon >

"Legal right." Merriam-Webster.com.
< https://www.merriam-webster.com/dictionary/legal%20right >

Levy, Jillian. "Moringa Benefits Hormonal Balance, Digestion, Mood, & More." Dr. Axe Food Is Medicine.
< https://draxe.com/moringa-benefits/#>

Lewis, Jessica. "What Are the Benefits of of Black Currant Tea?"Livestrong. <https://www.livestrong.com/article/254266-what-are-the-benefits-of-black-currant-tea/>

"Licorice Tea and Its Benefits." DrinkHerbalTea.com.
<https://www.drinkherbaltea.com/licorice-tea/>

"Linden Tea-The Healing Nectar." The Right Tea.
<https://www.therighttea.com/linden-tea.html>

"Linden (Tilia) Tea And Its Benefits."
https://www.drinkherbaltea.com/. < https://www.drinkherbal-tea.com/linden-tea-benefits/>

Marty, Erika. "Cinnamon Tea: Benefits for Heart and Immune Health Plus Potential Side Effects." Cup & Leaf.
< https://www.cupandleaf.com/blog/cinnamon-tea >

Marty, Erika. "LavenderTea Health Benefits, Side Effects, and How to Brew." Cup & Leaf.
< https://www.cupandleaf.com/blog/lavender-tea >

Mayo Clinic Staff. "Lupus." Mayo Clinic.
< https://www.mayoclinic.org/diseases-conditions/lupus/symptoms-causes/syc-20365789>

Mccarthy, Karen. "Benefits of Rosehip Tea."Livestrong.

<https://www.livestrong.com/article/23079-benefits-rosehip-tea/>

Mccarthy, Karen. "What Are the Health Benefits of Mulberry Leaf Tea?" Livestrong.
<https://www.livestrong.com/article/265868-what-are-the-health-benefits-of-mulberry-leaf-tea/>

Mccarthy, Karen. "Which Herbal Teas Are a D?" Livestrong.
<https://www.livestrong.com/article/138178-which-herbal-teas-are-diuretic/>

McDermott, Annette. "How to Make Sage Tea." Love to Know.
<https://herbs.lovetoknow.com/herbal-teas/how-make-sage-tea>

Monaco, Emily. "7 Healthy Benefits of Peppermint Tea: Are You Drinking Enough?" Organic Authority.
< https://www.organicauthority.com/energetic-health/5-fantastic-health-benefits-of-peppermint-tea >

McKeown, Marie. "Herbal Teas to Increase Energy Levels Naturally." CalorieBee.
<https://caloriebee.com/vitamins-supplements/Herbals-Teas-to-Increase-Energy-Levels-Naturally>

"Mulberry." California Rare Fruit Growers.
<https://www.crfg.org/pubs/ff/mulberry.html>

Murphy, Cheryl. "What Are the Health Benefits of Saffron Tea?"Livestrong.
<https://www.livestrong.com/article/172053-what-are-the-health-benefits-of-saffron-tea/>

Myszko, Amy. "What Kind of Tea Helps a Sinus Infection?"Livestrong.

<https://www.livestrong.com/article/199290-what-kind-of-tea-helps-a-sinus-infection/>

Nagdeve, Meenakshi. "11 Amazing Hibiscus Tea HealthBenefits." Organic Facts. <https://www.organicfacts.net/health-benefits/beverage/hibiscus-tea.html>

Nagdeve, Meenakshi. "11 Surprising Matcha Tea Benefits." OrganicFacts. <https://www.organicfacts.net/health-benefits/beverage/matcha-tea.html>

Nagdeve, Meenakshi. "13 Amazing Benefits of Red Rooibos Tea." Organic Facts. <https://www.organicfacts.net/health-benefits/beverage/health-benefits-of-red-rooibos-tea.html>

"Nettle Tea & Its Health Benefits" https://www.drinkherbaltea.com/. <https://www.drinkherbaltea.com/nettle-tea/>

Novak, Jess. "12 Teas That Boost Your Mood." The Daily Meal. <https://www.thedailymeal.com/drink/12-teas-boost-your-mood-slideshow>

Oijala, Leena. "Make Your Own Lung-Healing Herbal Tea with Mullein." Organic Authority. <https://www.organicauthority.com/health/mullein-herbal-tea>

Patil, Kiran. "Health Benefits & Nutrition of Peach." Organic Facts. < https://www.organicfacts.net/health-benefits/fruit/health-benefits-of-peach.html>

Patterson, Susan. "16 Reasons Why You Should Drink Echinacea Tea Every Day." Natural Living Ideas.

<https://www.naturallivingideas.com/echinacea-tea-benefits/>

"Peach Leaf Tea: Benefits, Side Effects, how to make." Herbal Teas Online.
< https://www.herbalteasonline.com/peach-tea.php >

"Pineapple Tea and Its Benefits."
https://www.drinkherbaltea.com/.
<https://www.drinkherbaltea.com/pineapple-tea-benefits/>

Porter, Lisa. "Herbal Tea & Iron." Livestrong.
<https://www.livestrong.com/article/467434-herbal-tea-iron/>

Rao, Jyotsana. "22 Amazing Benefits Of Chamomile Tea for Skin, Hair, and Health."
< https://www.stylecraze.com/articles/health-benefits-of-chamo-mile-tea/#gref >

"Red Clover Tea And Its Benefits." Drink Herbal Tea.com.
<https://www.drinkherbaltea.com/red-clover-tea/>

 Renee, Janet. "Teas That Lower Blood Sugar." Livestrong.
<https://www.livestrong.com/article/498295-teas-that-lower-blood-sugar/>

"Rosehip Tea: Amazing Source of Vitamin C." The Right Tea.
<https://www.therighttea.com/rosehip-tea.html>

Roulston, David. "Best Herbal Tea for Memory and Focus." Herbs for Health.
<https://www.herbs-for-health.com/tea-memory-and-focus/>

 S., Abi. "5 Herbal Teas To Boost Your Immune System." The Credible Choice.
<https://www.thecrediblechoice.com/how/herbal-teas-to-boost-

your-immune-system/>

Sewarad, Marc. "10 Science Backed Benefits of Rose Tea." Healthy Focus.
<https://healthyfocus.org/8-benefits-of-rose-tea/>

Shruti. "Cinnamon Tea and Benefits." Healthyy.
<https://healthyy.net/superfoods/why-cinnamon-tea-is-an-awe-some-energy-drink-and-how-to-prepare-it>

"Statistics About Diabetes." American Diabetes Association.
<http://www.diabetes.org/diabetes-basics/statistics/>

Staughton, John. "Benefits & Side Effects of Mullein Tea." Organic Facts. < https://www.organicfacts.net/mullein-tea.html >

Staughton, John. "Top 10 Benefits of Chrysanthemum Tea." Organic Facts.
<https://www.organicfacts.net/health-benefits/beverage/bene-fits-chrysanthemum-tea.html>

Staughton, John. "8 Surprising Benefits of Turmeric Ginger Tea." Organic Facts.
<https://www.organicfacts.net/health-benefits/herbs-and-spices/turmeric-ginger-tea.html >

Staughton, John. "8 Surprising Red Clover Benefits." Organic Facts.
<https://www.organicfacts.net/health-benefits/herbs-and-spices/red-clover.html >

Staughton, John. "9 Impressive Benefits of Vanilla." Organic Facts.
<https://www.organicfacts.net/health-benefits/herbs-and-spices/vanilla.html >

Staughton, John. "9 Health Benefits of Peppermint Tea." OrganicFacts.
<https://www.organicfacts.net/health-benefits/beverage/peppermint-tea.html >

Staughton, John. "15 Benefits of Chamomile Tea." Organic Facts.
<https://www.organicfacts.net/health-benefits/beverage/chamomile-tea-benefits-uses.html>

Staughton, John. "21 Amazing Benefits of Fennel Tea." Organic Facts.
<https://www.organicfacts.net/health-benefits/beverage/fennel-tea.html >

Staughton, John. "25 Amazing Benefits of Nettle Tea." OrganicFacts.
<https://www.organicfacts.net/health-benefits/beverage/nettle-tea.html>

The Herb Companion Staff. "Herb to Know: Mullein (Verbascum thapsus)." Mother Earth Living.
<https://www.motherearthliving.com/plant-profile/herb-to-know-mullein-verbascum-thapsus>

"Turmeric tea to start your day-Fight cancer and build your brain at the same time (with a flavor pro tip)." Fresh Bites Daily.
<https://www.freshbitesdaily.com/turmeric-tea/>

"Vanilla Benefits & Information." Herbwisdom.com.
<https://www.herbwisdom.com/herb-vanilla.html>

Vine, W.E.; Unger, Merrill F.; and William, White Jr. Vine's Complete Expository Dictionary of Old and New Testament Words, Nashville, TN: Thomas Nelson, Inc.

Ware, Megan. "What's to know about hibiscus tea?" Medical News Today.
<https://www.medicalnewstoday.com/articles/318120.php >

Watson, Stephanie. "The Effects of High Cholesterol on the Body." Healthline.
<https://www.healthline.com/health/cholesterol/effects-on-body#1>

"What is Lupus?" Lupus Foundation of America.
<https://www.lupus.org/resources/what-is-lupus >

"What is Ginger Tea?" Teatulia Organic Teas.
< https://www.teatulia.com/tea-varieties/what-is-ginger-tea.htm >

"What is Rooibos tea?" Teatulia Organic Teas.
< https://www.teatulia.com/tea-varieties/what-is-rooibos.htm>

"What is TulsiTea?" Teatulia Organic Teas.
< https://www.teatulia.com/tea-varieties/what-is-tulsi.htm >

Williams, Josh. "Herbal Tea for Bad Breath." Living HerbalTea.
<https://www.livingherbaltea.com/herbal-tea-bad-breath/>

Williams, Josh. "The Flavor of Chamomile Herbal Tea." LivingHerbal Tea.
< https://www.livingherbaltea.com/flavor-chamomile-herbal-tea/>

Wroblewski, M.T. "What is Sage Tea Good For?" SFGate.
<https://healthyeating.sfgate.com/sage-tea-good-for-8148.html>

Yaneff, Jon. "Hibiscus Tea: Health Benefits, Nutrition, Side Effects, and Recipes." Doctors Health Press.

.<https://www.doctorshealthpress.com/food-and-nutrition-articles/hibiscus-tea-benefits/>

Zak, Victoria. *20,000 Secrets of Tea: The Most Effective Ways to Benefit from Nature's Healing Herbs, New York*, NY: Dell Publishing. "

5 Benefits of Drinking Pineapple Peel Tea and How to Make It." Pineapple Company.
< https://pineapplecr.com/en/5-benefits-of-drinking-pineapple-peel-tea-and-how-tomake-it/>

"5 Ways Green Tea is Good for Your Oral Health." Best Health.
<https://www.besthealthmag.ca/best-you/oral-health/5-ways-green-tea-is-good-for-your-oral-health/>

"10 Reasons Why You Need Chrysanthemum Tea In Your Life."BeWellBuzz.
< https://www.bewellbuzz.com/wellness-buzz/10-health-benefits-chrysanthemum-tea/>

INDEX

A

Acne 18, 139
Alertness 8, 9, 82, 133
Allergic Reactions 117
Allergies 19, 111
Alzheimer's 117, 128
Anemia 154
Angelica Root tea 78
Anise tea 107
Antidepressant 68
Antioxidant 39, 64, 116
Anxiety 14, 82, 83, 93, 117, 139,
    140, 153
Arthritis 23, 68, 128
Asthma 88, 122, 142, 143, 154
Autoimmune Disease 23

B

Bad Breath 108, 112, 121, 122
Bamboo Leaf tea 59
Bilberry tea 93, 153
Bitter Orange tea 73
Black Currant tea 159
Black tea 9, 14, 92, 98, 127, 153
Blood Pressure 63, 64, 88, 152
Blood Sugar 73, 83, 152, 153
Bronchitis 28, 88, 122
Burdock tea 128

C

Calcium 9, 39, 103
Calendula tea 19, 143
Cancer 39, 68, 98, 121, 128, 164
Chamomile tea.....3, 34, 54, 68, 78,
    139, 148, 152, 153
Cholesterol 39, 54, 64, 73, 88, 93,
    128, 132, 133, 139
Chrysanthemum tea.....8, 13, 18,
    23, 28, 33, 38, 43, 48, 53, 58,
    63, 67, 72, 77, 82, 87, 92, 97,
    102, 107, 111, 116, 121, 127,
    132, 138, 142, 147, 152, 154,
    158, 163, 166, 167
Cinnamon tea 23, 159, 163
Cold 78
Concentration 116
Congestion 28, 29, 111
Conjunctivitis 107
cough 122
Coughing 28, 142

D

Damiana tea 83
Dandelion tea 88, 103, 148
Dementia 117
Depression 14, 117

Detox 87
Diabetes 24, 73, 133, 152
Diuretic 160
Dong Quai tea 73

E

Ear Infection 77
Echinacea tea 77, 78
Eczema 18, 127, 128
Elderberry tea 68, 112
Energy 1, 38, 72, 73, 133
Eyebright tea 93
Eyes .. 5, 6, 7, 15, 16, 22, 26, 36, 41,
    62, 75, 76, 79, 81, 91, 92, 98,
    107, 108, 113, 118, 119, 120,
    125, 126, 146

F

Fennel tea 107, 164
Fever 9, 77
Flu 28, 44, 67
Focus 5, 7, 8, 9, 15, 26, 61, 85, 124,
    125, 126
Fumitory tea 128

G

Ginger tea 39, 53, 54, 64, 112,
    122, 133, 139, 147
Ginkgo Biloba tea 116, 157
Ginseng tea 64, 134
Gotu Kola tea 117
Graviola tea 108
Green tea .. 9, 19, 38, 39, 64, 68, 73,
    98, 117, 123, 147, 148, 153

H

Hair 49, 58, 59, 139
Hawthorn tea 103

Headache 4, 43
Headaches 9, 19, 44, 83, 143
Heart Disease 68, 97, 98, 132
Heart Attack 97
Heartburn 28
Heat Stroke 9
Hibiscus tea 63, 64, 67, 133
Honeybush tea 33, 155, 156
Hormones 73, 143
Horsetail tea 58, 156, 158
Hyssop tea 54

I

Immune Booster 108
Immune System 19, 23, 24, 34, 49,
    67, 68, 78, 88, 107, 112, 128,
    133, 143, 148
Indigestion 14, 44, 83
Infections 44, 59, 67, 68, 77, 78,
    107, 111, 112, 133, 143, 152
Inflammation .. 23, 24, 53, 59, 103,
    107, 127, 128, 142, 143, 148
Insomnia 3, 14, 19
irritable bowel syndrome 29

J

joint pain 23, 24, 143

L

Lavender tea 13, 159
Lemon Balm tea 34, 83
Lemongrass tea 68, 147
Licorice tea 28, 34, 143
Linden tea 43, 159
lupus 23

M

magnesium 9, 93, 103

Marshmallow tea 54
Matcha tea 132, 161
Memory 154, 162
menopause 34
menstrual cramps 49
migraines 117
minerals 9, 39, 103
mood 11, 45, 73, 82, 147, 148
Moringa tea 72
motion sickness 112
Mulberry tea 38, 155
Mullein tea 142, 163
muscle cramps 29
muscle soreness 53

N

nausea 54, 112, 138, 139
Nettle tea 102, 161, 164

O

Oat Straw tea 59
Oolong tea 9, 14, 19, 153
Oral Health 166
osteoporosis 103

P

Parsley tea 88
Peach tea 92
Peppermint tea 111, 160, 164
Pineapple tea 24, 143, 147, 148
Plantain tea 88
prehypertension 63, 64

R

Red Clover tea 87, 162
Red Raspberry Leaf tea ... 103, 139
Redbush tea 133
Rooibos tea 18, 158

Rose tea 48, 163
Rosehip tea 24, 67, 68
Rosemary tea 44, 117

S

Saffron tea 49, 93, 97, 98
sinus 111, 112
skincare 18, 19
sleep 3, 33, 34, 153
sore throat 77
stomach ulcers 29
stomachaches 14, 78
stress 13, 14, 68, 73, 93, 97, 122, 153
stroke 132, 152
sunburns 18
swelling 23, 128

T

Thyme tea 49, 112
toothaches 9, 78
tranquility 13
Tulsi tea 14, 121, 122
Turmeric tea 98, 108, 127, 128, 164

U

ulcers 59, 121

V

Vanilla tea 39, 134, 138, 139
Vervain tea 83
vision 9, 5, 89, 92
Vitamin A 67, 92
Vitamin C 48, 49, 88, 147, 158, 162
vitamins 9, 48, 58, 67, 73

W

weight loss.............38, 39, 54, 148
White Pine tea 49
White Willow tea...................... 108
Wild Yam tea............................. 54

Y

Yarrow tea 78, 88
Yellow Dock tea 103

ABOUT THE AUTHOR

Andria Singletary was born and raised in Southern California. She graduated from California State University, San Bernardino with her Bachelor's Degrees in Psychology and Human Development and her Master's Degree in Child Development. Andria has worked in the early childhood field for the past seven years. She currently works as a Program Director for a preschool that caters to both typically developing and medically fragile children. Andria first fell in love with writing at the young age of 12. It wasn't until her early 20s that she began to share her writing with the world through her blog, Sweetly Broken. Andria attended and served at Abundant Living Family Church for nine years. During that time, she served in the young adult ministry and children's ministry. Andria recently started attending Elevate Life Church and still resides in Southern California with her loving husband Antoine Singletary.

CPSIA information can be obtained
at www.ICGtesting.com
Printed in the USA
LVHW050911130721
692556LV00002B/85